Pivot Point

How to Turn on a Dime
Without Sacrificing Results

SHAWN RHODES

DEDICATION

This book is dedicated to the men and women in uniform around the world who create Pivot Points every day,
all so we can have the freedom to create them in ours.

OUTLINE

PREFACE

I f you're like most of the leaders and business owners I know, then you've opened this book with one question in mind:

> "I've got about ten seconds to spend working on my business before I get back to dealing with employees, customers and the thousand other things I juggle every day. What are you going to tell me in that amount of time that will make my organization better?"

That's a tall order, and I accept the challenge.

This should take about ten seconds to read and will answer your question:

In your life and in your business, the best plans never work out as planned. The biggest need I hear from the companies I work with – and this is backed up by reams of research – is a need for a way to proactively adapt – to pivot, if you will – whenever unexpected change occurs, wherever it occurs in your organization. This book is about creating a Pivot Point in your business. If you or your people are struggling with keeping up in a rapidly-changing environment, if you're tired of not meeting your business objectives or sliding in just under the wire, then you're ready to create a Pivot Point.

That's what this book is about. If creating such an organization interests you, read on.

INTRODUCTION

I'll start by defining what a Pivot Point is.

Pivot Point: A place where change not only should happen,
but must occur in order for a plan to be successful.
Additionally, it's the center point of a rotational system.

In organizations, a Pivot Point is not only the place and time where leaders, managers and employees shift in their way of getting things done; it's also the turning point that allows change to happen quickly. If you've worked for or within organizations, then you know how painfully change occurs – and you also know how needed change sometimes doesn't occur at all.

According to the news, our economy is slowly recovering from our last major recession. Real estate values are on the rise for the first time in half a decade, and companies are reporting record profits again. However, those in business are experiencing something different. While they may be making a profit, their costs are rising. Technology is improving the way we get things done, but the focus of employees is being pulled in a thousand different directions, lowering actual productivity. Additionally, some industries are experiencing growth but others are in decline. Fortune. com reported that the number of factories in the US has dropped 15% since 2001. And while many companies are reporting record revenues, Bloomberg tells us consumer spending is at the lowest it's been since 2009. All of this paints a dismal picture for businesses that are trying to do more with less.

In just the last few years, Wet Seal, Circuit City and Caesar's Entertainment – some of the most profitable businesses in their given industries – have failed. With a corporation failing every 3 minutes and another filing for bankruptcy every 8 minutes, our modern economy has claimed some businesses that were stalwarts in their industries. Why did these and similar organizations, once at the top of their markets, succumb to rapid change? I believe it's because they didn't shift. They didn't do old things in a new way, a way that took advantage of the change they were experiencing. In short, they didn't pivot.

"By Failing to Prepare, You Are Preparing to Fail"

The above quote is most often attributed to Benjamin Franklin, and it's even more applicable when looking at why something fails. Each of the organizations that have declared bankruptcy in the last decade had competitors that not only survived, but thrived as a result of capitalizing on changes in technology, their markets, customer demand, industry regulations and a host of other causes. These successful companies were able to rapidly change the way they did business in order to stay a step ahead of the changes they saw coming (or the changes that took them by surprise). Simply stated – they had a plan that took advantage of the changes that occurred. And yet the companies that have failed also had plans; they also had some of the brightest minds in leadership and in business consulting advising them. What did the successful ones do differently? What set them apart from their peers that went the way of the dodo?

THE 5 DEADLY MISTAKES COMPANIES MAKE

Rather than looking at what successful companies did that allowed them to survive, it may be more helpful to look at what they didn't do. What they didn't do was make the same strategic mistakes that most companies make each and every day. These mistakes are the slow, insidious killers of organizations and the very things that prevent Pivot Points from being created. Once we understand these strategic mistakes, it will be easy to see the need for having an organization that can pivot and rapidly respond to change.

Mistake #1: Believing Better Strategies = Better Results

It's a fact that businesses are overwhelmed with demands – the chief of which is to turn a profit. Unfortunately, only focusing on generating revenue prevents many companies from making the very changes that allow them to innovate, adapt and survive. According to a study published in the *Harvard Business Review*, only 15% of the 197 large companies surveyed actually reviewed the results they achieved against their plans. While it may seem like a no-brainer that we can't manage what we don't measure, 85% of the companies surveyed are all making the same critical mistake – not looking back over their results. The best strategies in the world mean nothing if they are not measured and cannot be replicated.

What does that mean to a company's bottom line? If we don't know where we are getting the greatest return in our investment of time and capital, it's likely that underperforming projects will continue to receive support instead of being critically examined for improvement. Keep in mind that 'underperforming' doesn't necessarily mean 'unprofitable.' But without looking back and measuring results, there's no way to know if a project is as profitable as it could be.

Mistake #2: Working Smarter, Not Harder

Let's say that an organization is one of the rare 15% that does look back and measure their results. The next question is: What happens with the information learned? It has become common practice to accept sub-standard results in many organizations. In the same HBR-published study, it was found that most plans delivered only 63% of their projected return (while some leaders place the number closer to 50%)! That means even the best and brightest companies are leaving 37% of their possible revenue on the table. How is it possible that shareholders and leaders tolerate that much profit going out the door? As we learned in Strategic Mistake #1, because most companies don't measure results against projections, they can't make improvements. For the few that do measure results, **even fewer take action on what they learn.** They mistakenly believe that working smarter means constantly looking for the next best innovation. Unfortunately, skipping over the 'hard' work of actually examining results and implementing changes causes a chain reaction of diminished performance.

In this downward performance spiral, organizations come to expect sub-standard returns on their plans and strategies, creating a culture of underperformance.

Mistake #3: Believing *People* Drive Performance

Closely linked with Mistakes #1 and #2, a lack of monitoring results against projections creates massive bottlenecks inside companies. When we don't look at our performance, we don't know whether our results came from bad planning, incorrect strategy, incompetent employees, a combination of these issues, or a different reason altogether. The Society for Human Resource Management reports only 3 of 10 companies believe they are actively tracking performance from their employees. Because most organizations don't take the time to clearly assign accountabilities for performance, it's never clear who is responsible for not executing on their objectives. Companies mistakenly believe that hiring the best and brightest ensures they have people with good follow-through. As any experienced leader can tell you, education and intelligence are no guarantee of exceptional performance.

The only option this mistaken belief leaves is to base future growth on last year's numbers, because the only reliable metric to plan performance around is past performance. This leaves companies between a rock and a hard place. The best-case scenario in an organization that runs like that is a mere continuation of the current rate of growth. In contrast, high-performing organizations are constantly looking at where they *want* to be and then arranging the resources they'll need to get there. They don't put the cart before the horse.

So far, we've only been addressing the strategic mistakes that involve a company reviewing their results in an organized way. However, as many Six Sigma practitioners can attest, speeding up a broken system, whether human or mechanical, just produces more broken results. The most critical (and costly) strategic mistake most organizations make doesn't occur after the results are in — it happens before the plan is even launched.

Mistake #4: Believing Strategy Should Drive Performance

A company can have everything going for it — the best and brightest leadership, the most experienced advisors, passionate and dedicated employees, a product or service that was light-years ahead of the closest competitors' offering — and still not achieve their projected results. They count on a solid, well-planned strategy to carry the organization. The strategy sits on a shelf, or buried in a computer file, and people continue on with business as usual. These companies are making the mistake of not using performance — past, present and future — to create and drive their strategy's execution.

The most effective strategies in the world will fail when they aren't understood and acted upon. Often, the plan is understood by the leadership team, but the actions needed to execute it are lost in translation between the boardroom and the factory floor, or between one department and another.

This is the most effective way to take an otherwise brilliant strategy and destroy any chance it has to succeed.

As we've seen in the previously-covered strategic mistakes, it is *performance* that actually drives the execution of strategy, whether we want it to be that way or not.

Mistake #5: Tearing Down Silos

I can already hear the grumblings on this one – *"Wait, we've spent the last twenty years trying to tear down silos and improve communication! You want us to create more bureaucracy and layers of communication?!?"*

Not quite. While improving communication and reducing bureaucracy are great practices for any organization, most leaders jumped on this philosophy without mitigating the unintended results. Specifically, without an overarching planning and execution process – usually developed and driven by executives in a vertically-oriented organization – leaders across departments are left to their own devices when translating strategy into objectives, as well as executing on those objectives and tracking results.

The outcomes of this mistake are evident when leaders take a stroll onto the factory floor or ride along with a client-facing employee and ask, 'What are the company's strategic goals this year/quarter? What specific, measurable objectives are you executing and how do they tie into that overall strategy?' Most employees at *any* level of an organization will be unable to answer those questions, and yet those are the very questions that ensure alignment, performance and measurable growth for an organization.

HOW COMPANIES CURRENTLY DEAL WITH
UNEXPECTED CHANGE

Of course, businesses have known about the need to plan and react to change for as long as we've been trading shekels for animal hides. However, each of the aforementioned strategic mistakes stem from companies spending most of their time *reacting* to unexpected disruptions to their plans. A plethora of systems arose to address the need to connect strategy to execution and iteratively improve operations. Waterfall Planning, Agile, Six Sigma, Kanban and the Balanced Scorecard each represent processes that have sprung up to better prepare companies to execute their objectives, track performance and pivot when needed without losing momentum. The issue with all of the existing methodologies available is they are designed to work inside a fundamentally flawed planning and execution process. As we've gone over, when used inside a broken system, the best processes in the world just produce more broken results. What organizations need is a way to optimize not only their project's execution, but also their planning, preparation and ultimately, their continuous improvement. And until recently, that is something businesses have been unable to achieve.

The inability to find a cure to the most prevalent illness affecting organizations is due to the fact that they're just too busy handling day-to-day operations. For this reason, most choose to do nothing. Again, the best result they can expect with such a practice is continuing their current rate of growth. For some companies, that's enough. Each of the large companies that failed in the last decades believed last year's way of doing business was enough to ensure their survival. Time, the economy and their competitors proved them wrong.

For those few organizations that do see the writing on the wall, most choose to look internally for solutions. They've invested a lot in hiring capable and competent leaders – surely those individuals will have the answers that will close the gap between planning and performance. Unfortunately, most leaders are trained in business schools and their experience is in businesses all making the same strategic mistakes. Such settings train them to look through the lens of existing methods and resources, thereby leaving their solutions constricted by the very system they are trying to improve. Some organizations with the budget and foresight needed to proactively respond to change bring in the best outside help available – the titans of business consulting who make it their business to know the best practices of organizations across a wide array of industries. While information about the rate of consulting projects that fail is spotty at best, some sources place the rate of failure between 25% and 80%. Many consulting firms have specialties, but few focus solely on strategic planning and execution. Fewer still take the time to examine the goals that are feasible for their clients instead of relying on industry averages. And those that concern themselves with building solutions that enhance company culture and morale are particularly rare. Yet the very business model of large consulting firms requires they make clients dependent on their services – not a favorable place to be when you're the one that has to approve multi-million dollar consulting retainers. Any industry that helps more than it harms should be applauded, but the questions remain: How do we create organizations that can pivot when needed, that can respond to change and permanently avoid the strategic mistakes that so many organizations make? How do we create a Pivot Point in an organization?

SEARCHING FOR A BETTER SOLUTION

Over the last decade, I've studied Pivot Points in organizations all over the world by working with companies ranging from mom-and-pop businesses to those in the Fortune 100. Each of them faced similar challenges when it came to their Pivot Points. Despite size and revenue differences, Fortune 100 companies and small, family-run businesses have a lot in common – both are trying to keep the lights on. Both have shareholders to please, whether those are stockholders, employees or clients. Both have to concern themselves with competition and a volatile economy. More than anything else, every company, no matter what business they're in, has to plan for where they want to go and then try their best to get there in an ever-changing environment.

It's an old adage: no plan ever works out as planned. Whether this is due to complex environments or the complexity of humans interacting together, it's still a fact – plans inevitably change in any organization. One company may be dealing with a massive corporate merger while another is struggling to solve a delay in shipping their products, but it doesn't change their need to be nimble and remain flexible enough to respond to last-minute shifts. An organization that can't rapidly respond to changes, or pivot, **is destined to be overtaken by those that can.**

Recognizing that changes were costing organizations productivity and profit, an entire industry popped up in an attempt to make organizations nimbler, abler to respond to change. Countless books have been written to address the need to be flexible – books on strategic planning, personality types and leadership styles – all in an effort to create order in what is, by its very nature, a chaotic environment. Judging from the number of books released each year on those subjects, there's no lack of need to gain control – in any measure – when it seems like the train is going off the proverbial tracks. Unfortunately, many of the methods and techniques that fill the business section at every bookstore are attempting to wrestle a wild beast into submission by changing how leaders and employees react to change. And they work – just as long as people always apply them to the same problem that hopefully occurs in the same way every time. That's also why these methods never last and why new ones are released each month – not only is each problem unique, but when humans become overwhelmed, they revert back to survival mode and focus on getting the next task done. These methods and systems fail not because they are flawed – many are produced by some of the most brilliant minds in their industries. They fail because they're not addressing the root of the problem we covered earlier: businesses making strategic mistakes that *prevent* any new processes from working as well as they should.

The problem occurs in organizations when everyone is doing what they can to help the organization succeed in the best way they know how, not necessarily in the way that best serves the organization's strategic goals. What this creates is an organization full of highly-capable people, each pulling on their own end of the rope, wondering why getting things done, inter-departmentally and in their own teams, is so difficult. Leadership then steps in with the latest system, assessment or fad in an attempt to iron out the problem that is currently costing the organization the most resources. Leadership knows that things have to change, and like doctors, they do what they've been trained to do – fix the problem causing the most pain. This method of planning (and management) turns into a game of whack-a-mole, targeting the next problem in an attempt to change how the organization gets things done, whether that's to increase revenue, improve efficiency, or whatever the biggest challenge at the moment happens to be. If you've ever been a leader in such an organization, you know what a massive amount of resources this requires, and you know it produces sub-standard results. Few leaders take the time to look at what is stopping their organizations from being able to pivot when needed, as often as needed, without losing their effectiveness. Rather than simply changing the way things are managed when challenges arise (when deadlines are looming and everyone is running around with their hair on fire), leaders need to understand bandages won't heal the virus that's actually infecting their businesses.

When I interviewed CEOs of organizations, they all saw a need to get ahead of problems before they occurred, before those problems affected business metrics. They wanted a system, an execution process that was built to withstand last-minute changes. A system made for the most challenging environments in business. Such a system is what allows organizations to rapidly pivot and still meet their obligations to their stakeholders, and for the companies I worked with, it was as elusive as a unicorn.

Unless your organization is working with unchanging demands, being able to rapidly change direction is not only something you need to know how to do, it's necessary for your organization's survival. And it doesn't come from applying duct-tape to mitigate your problems. If you're like most leaders, you've likely been doing that for some time just to get by. It's not impossible to achieve goals using that method (it's what most companies do by default), but it does mean that you and your team are not getting the results you're truly capable of. Likely, you're looking for a way to stay a step ahead of your competition, align your employees around a common goal, empower your people to innovate solutions and continually improve how they get things done. In an environment like that, you know if a new challenge comes along, your people will be ready to proactively deal with it and change direction while still moving towards your business objectives. At the same time, you probably aren't looking to invest in complicated process-management software, re-vamp your culture, bring in a cadre of high-priced consultants to generate efficiency studies and market-trends analysis or completely reorganize your management structure.

And you shouldn't have to.

The type of organization I'm describing, the one that can nimbly pivot, is not a pipe dream. We've each seen elements of it in the places we've worked, but likely never all in one company.

The last-minute changes everyone experiences in a business environment are an inevitable part of working in complex systems – and there are few systems as complex as teams of people working in the challenging and changing landscape of modern business. As I began investigating what allowed high-performing organizations to pivot, I always found a few groups of people able to effortlessly change direction mid-stride. They were able to shift internal resources to meet customer demands, integrate new team members and see outside the blinders that many mid-level and front line employees tend to have. Such actions enabled them to sometimes completely scrap their original plan while still achieving their goals. These teams usually occur in small pockets; in my experience, they never exist across an entire company. When I interviewed these teams in businesses, I found something interesting – team leaders couldn't pin their high performers' success to a consciously-implemented process. As a researcher, this was incredibly frustrating. I was looking for a formula that could be replicated and I was repeatedly told one didn't exist. It was as if these high-performing teams, composed of just the right amount of personality and ambition, magically came together and executed in a way others couldn't. So instead of businesses benefitting from the same results their high-performers could reach, they had to settle for a few high-performing teams and funnel valuable resources into other teams in an attempt to raise performance. I began asking myself: Why isn't every team able to pivot like these rare high-performers?

It's the holy grail of process management and leadership – a system that raises the ability of everyone to that of their highest performer.

However, before I began studying businesses, I did see this level of pivot-ability occur across an entire organization. In this organization, I worked alongside hundreds of thousands of people who were masters of executing in challenging environments. My role in this organization was to study the very thing businesses spend billions of dollars a year to create – an organization-wide Pivot Point. You likely know someone in your family, neighborhood or community who has worked for this organization, though you may not know they were masters of creating the very thing businesses try so hard to achieve – a *Pivot Point*.

PART I:
The Mission and
The Business

The author, taken at Forward Operating Base St. Michael,
Mahmudiyah, Iraq in 2004.

A GLOBAL STUDY OF PIVOT POINTS

While most high school graduates are spending their first days away from home attending a university or looking for an internship, my first job was on a battlefield – literally. Instead of taking the route my peers did by finding work in the Appalachian town where we lived or heading off to college, I joined the Marine Corps. At 18, when my friends were running cash registers or stocking shelves, I was given the unique task of studying modern heroes - men and women on the front lines of combat. After completing basic training along with fellow Marines, I was taught to write and capture images that would form case studies of people who could pivot in the most challenging environments on the planet. For the next four years, my job was to travel with Marine Corps units to some of the most dangerous places in the world. I lived and fought alongside them, a notepad in one hand and a rifle in the other – learning what allowed them to be successful, what allowed them to pivot when most people would simply give up and go home.

I captured stories that changed history – the liberation of Baghdad, the first democratic elections in Iraq. I also captured the stories that simply changed the lives of the people involved – bringing medicine to sick children who had never seen a doctor, the reuniting of a father and son in the desert thousands of miles from home. As a Marine Corps War

Correspondent, I was able to share the stories of these remarkable men and women through two combat tours in Iraq and throughout missions across two dozen countries. Because I was embedded within military units, I was sent places that many civilian reporters refused to go or weren't allowed. The stories and photos I captured were shared around the world in international, national and local news outlets. While I enjoyed the exciting life of accompanying modern-day warriors on their missions, I always wondered what it was that allowed them to go into a situation without enough resources, against superior forces, in an ever-changing environment, with low chances of success and pivot as a cohesive team to get the job done – and get the job done they did. Our success rate was close to 100%, a figure that any organization would kill for and one that left our competitors in the dust. What was it that allowed these men and women to be successful when so many people with superior educations and resources seemed to struggle so much to accomplish their goals? There was a system at work within the military that allowed these groups to do what many would consider impossible. Each of the people and events I wrote about gave me a piece of the puzzle, but for years I didn't see how the pieces fit together.

I was asking the same question many business leaders ask their teams: What allows an organization to leverage unexpected change? It wasn't until I began working within and with businesses as a consultant that I saw an answer emerge. I transitioned from studying Marines on the front lines to helping companies execute their strategies in a better way. Strangely, it was seeing organizations suffer from those 5 strategic mistakes that showed me how the puzzle pieces from the military fit together. I was able to sit in the boardrooms of Fortune 100 companies and hear their executives plan strategy. I was able to be on the front lines when their employees were face-to-face with customers executing that same strategy. What was missing in the organizations I worked with was a process that was universally understood and practiced from the executive suite down to the customer-facing employees. If success came, the companies did it in spite of themselves, and their leaders freely admitted as much. Whether their business objective was a small one or a multi-national endeavor, businesses always seemed like they slid into home plate just milliseconds before the ball hit the catcher's mitt. What this meant was they were not maximizing the effectiveness of the resources the company invested in its training, equipment and people. In addition, as soon as the goal was met, the teams were immediately thrown into executing the next objective. Rarely did anyone take the time to find out what had gone wrong – or right – and build that into their next plan.

I realized the men and women I saw on the battlefield were successful in pivoting because each of them was part of a planning and execution process understood and practiced by team members at all levels of their organization. It wasn't a process only pulled out for their 'stretch' goals, because in combat, every mission is a stretch goal. Instead this process was instituted even for the seemingly mundane tasks that had to be accomplished every day – whether it was equipment maintenance, upgrade training or filing paperwork. While no member of the military is expected to be fluent in all levels of the process (generals have little use in knowing how to break down and clean crew-served weapons, while machine-gunners have little need for campaign planning), each of them is well-trained in the parts of the process that affect their performance. And believe it or not, the duties of a service member have a lot in common with those of an employee in a company. A major challenge is dealing with last-minute changes to the plan – when the environment changes, organizations have to pivot to be successful, whether their service is designing software or providing global defense.

I've personally witnessed this pivot-ability around the world through my participation in hundreds of missions, many of them in combat. In all of those missions, whether the Marines I was with were training or executing in some of the most dangerous environments on earth, I never saw one go completely as planned. If no mission went exactly as planned, how were they able to achieve a near 100% success rate? These men and women were not only used to pivoting, to responding to last-minute changes; they built methods for dealing with those changes into their planning and execution processes.

This process, this way of getting business done, stands in contrast to the band aid solutions many organizations use in an attempt to react to change. Instead of waiting for something in their plan to change, the military plans for how they will respond to changes before they occur. This allows them to get ahead of their competition, seize market share and win – To Pivot.

Once I pieced together the elements of pivoting, I began looking back on all the individual processes I'd seen at work on battlefields around the world. Of course, the military is full of high-performing teams. Excellence isn't a goal for these men and women – it's the standard they're held to. But like their civilian counterparts, they aren't born knowing how to execute at a high level. They are taught the processes and techniques that make them successful in stressful environments with limited resources. And like the planning and execution processes that serve men and women in the military, these processes apply to executing business objectives as well.

Much like the military, businesses have strategies and goals. Like the men and women I served alongside, companies have limited resources and time. More than anything, both business and military units are operating in environments that change just as fast as they plan for them. Each has to deal with maintaining shareholder support and competing for funds with an overstretched budget while continuing to produce more with less. Yet, military units are able to take a group of people with sometimes just a few months of training and little higher education, and then get them to work together as a team, not just in the air-conditioned office but where the rubber meets the road – in executing their missions. This was the opposite of the way I saw most businesses operate, even those that recruited employees from Ivy League schools and had billions of dollars in resources. When the going got tough, their plans crumbled and their profitability suffered. For many companies, when the environments they are working in change, whether through economic conditions, supply-chain problems, or customer demands, a mad scramble ensues to keep their teams on track toward their goals.

While business leaders have become used to dealing with changing environments, only recently have they begun to quantify the costs of not meeting their projected profitability. As we've learned, studies found many organizations are operating at 63% of their projected profitability. In an environment where many budgets are created on projected revenue, it's no wonder most businesses are happy to accept being a hair ahead of their competition as long as they come out on top.

Obviously, that strategy wouldn't work for the military. 'Barely winning' means a lot of good people aren't going home to their families. To convince a group of 18-24 year-olds to step into an environment with the 50%-or-greater mortality rate which exists in urban warfare, military leaders have to use a planning and execution process that eases anxiety and inspires confidence. From generals to the privates on the front lines, each person understands what the overall goal is, where their individual mission fits into that strategy and what resources they have available to accomplish their objectives. Only when all these things are made clear can people confidently walk into a challenging environment not with the knowledge that they have a chance of success – but with the belief that success is already theirs.

That's a belief that business leaders want instilled in their people – and a belief that they invest a lot of resources in creating. From multi-billion dollar businesses to social movements, leaders are always looking for a way to emotionally engage their employees and supporters around their missions. And from Patrick Lencioni to Steven Covey, a whole industry has arisen on how to craft mission statements and programs that drive action and alignment. However, a clear mission statement without a clear process for accomplishing it when the plan inevitably changes means an organization of passionate people that consistently pivot in opposite directions. When conditions change, people will continue to push toward whatever short-term goal they have without considering whether that goal is still relevant or aligned to their organization's long-term strategy.

So how does an organization get the best of all worlds – passionate employees, stellar execution, and the ability to change direction when the environment dictates? How can organizations create a Pivot Point that not only empowers employees to execute the company's goals, but also get better every single day? That is the focus of this book. As the world of business becomes simultaneously smaller from globalization and more complicated with a generational changing-of-the-guard and changing technology, there is a need for a common way of planning strategy and executing. There is a need for a process that allows companies to respond to change not as a leadership gimmick or short-term solution, but as the way they operate their businesses day-to-day. Each organization has an opportunity to decide to roll with change – not in the way they react to challenges, but in the way they plan for change before it ever arises. It's a turning point in the way business gets done; a Pivot Point that doesn't slow down results, but accelerates them.

THE FOUR P'S OF PIVOT POINT

Because the lessons of Pivot Point are taken from the missions I witnessed on both the battlefield and in businesses across America, I have included the lessons that create a Pivot Point as part of a story I covered as an embedded Marine Corps War Correspondent. It was one of the most dangerous missions I saw attempted: a small patrol of Marines that went alone into the heart of Fallujah in 2004 and miraculously returned without a single casualty. Each of the lessons that will allow you to increase your organization's pivot-ability is told from the perspective of a Marine that participated in a mission that no one was expected to survive. After the stories of this patrol, you will see how the principles they used apply in business environments. These are examples of how the same systems are used in the business world, taken from situations where businesspeople actually used the processes in order to increase their market share and bottom-line revenue, respond to last-minute changes and continue to improve their day-to-day operations. At the end of the book is a 'field guide' so that you, the leader or manager of your team, can introduce and apply each of the four P's of Pivot Point in a way that allows you to capitalize on changes you'll inevitably encounter.

THE FOUR P'S OF CREATING A PIVOT POINT: PLAN, PREPARE, PERFORM, PROCESS

Plan

One of the biggest needs any organization has is aligning their people around a common goal. The military is no different. Before military leaders send their troops into harm's way, they assess all the last-minute changes they're likely to face and plan around a shared objective, one that is communicated to all levels of leadership. This communication doesn't just include the objectives of particular missions, but also includes how their missions fit together into an overall strategy. The military's plans are specific, down to the time and day and hour of their execution. Although they know that no plan survives contact with the enemy, they also understand the more specific they are the better their chances of success.

Unfortunately, many organizations spend little time planning how they will accomplish their goals or dealing with inevitable changes to their plans. It doesn't have to be that way. In the military, because so much rides on the effectiveness execution, they are serious about planning. Rather than it being something that is seen as a chore, combat leaders understand their level of performance is directly proportionate to the amount of time they spend planning their missions. Because they plan before their troops step out the gate, they have time to examine all the resources they have available and on-call, line them up and establish 'trigger events' for when those resources will be called into play, either as part of their planned mission or when contingencies arise. Before these leaders leave their planning room, they know exactly who will be responsible for accomplishing each part of their mission. This person is a 'single-point-of-accountability,' and they are the ones that bring the mission objective to their sub-team. A similar planning process occurs until everyone – even in an organization of hundreds of thousands of people – knows exactly what role they will play and when they will be called upon to play it. This is much more than most businesses even consider doing – and it's a key factor in their inability to pivot.

Most people think with that much time invested in planning, they should be able to launch their teams right into action and get stellar results. However, military leaders wouldn't dream of sending their troops out the front gate to execute their missions yet. They still have to:

Prepare

Each member of the sub-missions – the 'execution teams' – gets together before they leave the safe confines of their forward-operating base, not to wish each other good luck, but to go over their part of the plan. This is not a question-and-answer session, but rather a pre-mission briefing. Their team leader gives them an overview of how what they're about to do fits into the overall strategy. The leader also goes over the potential problems they might face and what resources are lined up to deal with them – should the problems arise. This key step is a surefire way to re-align teams and to make them aware of the most likely changes they'll encounter. Each member of the team acknowledges what role they will play throughout the mission, and finally, the team goes over what could go wrong and what they'll do if it does. The whole process takes less than 10 minutes, but saves time, money and lives when they step into the next part of the process, where they go out to accomplish their objectives:

Perform

This is where the rubber meets the road – both in the military and in business – the concrete actions that drive the organization toward its goal. Everyone has a lot to do and not much time to do it, and people can become overwhelmed with everything going on around them. This is the most common point of failure when unexpected change occurs. In the military, processes have been developed that keep first things first and ensure that the primary objective is achieved. Troops on the ground train in these processes so that when they are 'client-facing,' they can rely on muscle memory and still perform at an extremely high level no matter how much their original plan changes.

Like those in the business world, our service men and women have a lot to accomplish with limited resources. They have to know how much ammunition they have, how long their support will take to arrive and how to shift their duties when a specialized skill is needed. Additionally, they have to have a way to manage the feeling of being overwhelmed that comes with stress, tight timelines and last-minute changes. When the mission is over and the team is back at their base, they may be tired, dirty and bloody, but they don't hit the showers quite yet. Their final step is to:

Process

One of the key factors that makes the military such a high-performing organization – one that can rapidly learn from mistakes and replicate innovation – is that after every mission, the team takes time to process what happened. In the military, this is referred to as an after-action report. While it's incredibly useful as a continuous-improvement process, it also ensures lessons will be passed on to the next generation.

Currently, many businesses are concerned with how they will handle the leadership turnover that accompanies a changing-of-the-guard between millennials and baby boomers. Recognizing the inevitable turnover of its people, the military developed a process for transferring organizational knowledge. With almost 20% of the entire Marine Corps turning over each year (other branches experience similar turnover rates), they can't afford not to capture best practices and standardize their operations. After every mission, Marines step into an after-action meeting to examine what happened, enabling them to learn from their wins and reduce or eliminate their failures. Some businesses know these types of meetings as 'debriefs' or 'post-mortems.' Whatever they're called, they are rarely used and even more rarely practiced as a continuous improvement process in organizations. For those that do, it is how they stay a step ahead of their competition, how they continue to innovate at a rate their competition can't begin to match and how they conquer unforeseen changes.

Before Getting Started

What you are about to read are the stories of men and women in uniform and in business, stories that were told to me or that I witnessed firsthand on the battlefield of Iraq and in businesses. As a war correspondent, I was allowed into the planning sessions of senior officers and was then sent to the front lines to see those plans in action. Because I am bringing together elements of planning and execution that affect both leaders and client-facing personnel, the system you will learn is unique both to the military and the world of business – very few people in combat or in corporations ever see a comprehensive view of the processes that make service members able to pivot so successfully. Each of the 4 P's of Pivot Point that you will learn can be implemented on their own to great effect in your organization to eliminate or mitigate changes that are currently affecting your bottom line. Or, for maximum result, they can be used together so your entire team can leverage the wisdom of your high performers, execute at an even higher level and 'bring everyone home' to reach your company's objectives. I recommend reading all the stories and then digging into the field guide to adapt this method to your organization's goals and daily execution. You can then read through the military and business examples as needed when a refresher is desired.

This isn't a new way of doing business for many high-performing leaders, but it is a different way of getting things done. As you read through the stories, you'll see the same challenges you likely face in your organization – both in the military and business examples. By the end of the book, you'll have a better understanding of how some of the most incredible men and women on Earth are able to accomplish some extremely challenging goals. You'll also have a clear path to achieve the goals your organization is aiming for.

Finally, get ready to pivot …

PLAN

Photo By Cpl. Matthew Manning, USMC

THE MISSION: PLAN, PART I

June 8, 2004
Camp Fallujah, Iraq

As Captain Barclay ducked his head to walk between the parted canvas tent flaps, a quote from one of his instructors at Officer Candidate School rang through his head: "No plan survives contact with the enemy."

That always made Barclay smile. It had also served him well in his nine years of military service, years that took him from Officer Candidate School in Quantico, VA, to flight school where he learned to fly helicopters. In his first leadership position in Cherry Point, NC, he learned it was true even when he wasn't fighting an 'enemy.' In hundreds of flights and training missions, none had gone exactly as planned. Whether it was due to old equipment or the hundreds of tasks that had to be accurately performed in every mission, adapting to change became a way of life.

Barclay learned to repeat the quote to himself often, especially when he was stepping into a planning session, like he was today. If military leaders liked to do anything, they liked to plan. Barclay wasn't a professional planner, he was a helicopter pilot. But because air combat gave coalition forces an advantage over their enemy, Barclay and his team were often

31

called into planning sessions to lend their insight. When his squadron commander informed him he was expected to be at these planning session (requests weren't usually made – officers were 'expected' at events rather than requested to them), Barclay knew it was going to be an interesting experience. There was a buzz around the tent that served as the planning room and sometimes 'officer's club' within Camp Fallujah. Something big was in the works, and the leaders of units all over their area of operations were being called in to attend the session at the compound the Marines called home.

Barclay paused for a minute inside the cramped tent and let his eyes adjust to the dim light. Outside in the Iraqi desert, the sun reflected from the dirt and sand, creating a convection-like heat that was currently topping 117 degrees Fahrenheit. The change in environment from the humid coast of North Carolina to the Middle East had taken time for him and the others to adjust to, but the Corps learned this lesson in the early 1800s in Africa. There, a lieutenant had crossed the Saharan desert on foot and conquered the city of Tripoli. His trek was legendary, and the lessons he learned about surviving in a desert environment had been passed down generation after generation. Barclay's water intake was monitored every day, and even the officers were constantly encouraged to monitor themselves for signs of heatstroke.

Barclay turned in the tent and found himself standing beside other uniformed personnel, some wearing flight suits like him, others in the pale brown and cream-patterned digital camouflage of ground-combat Marines. A few electric bulbs hung from the ceiling, giving off their incandescent light in the dark green structure. The spartan décor was complemented by a table in the center of the tent where topographical maps of the nearby city Fallujah were laid. Other, more narrow tables lined the walls of the room where personnel worked at computers to monitor operations that stretched over hundreds of square miles. A modern air conditioner steadily hummed, fighting a futile battle to cool the cramped, oven-like space. Barclay looked around the medium-sized tent and recognized the other officers and senior non-commissioned officers that made up his task force – Marines assembled from all over the world to deploy together as a cohesive unit. Most of them had never met before this deployment, but because they all used the same processes for dealing with unexpected change, they were able to come together at a moment's notice and operate like they had been working together for years.

Barclay grabbed the Velcro flap across his chest and exhaled with relief as he peeled the layers back from his protective vest. The Velcro emitted a loud rip as it separated, exposing Barclay's sweat-stained torso through the flight suit he wore. The sweat that immediately dried in the desert heat on his body was trapped under the flak vest he wore from morning until night. Barclay unbuckled his helmet strap, lifting the helmet off a head of tightly-cropped hair that all male Marines were required to wear, and set his gear against an open space on the wall of the tent. Each of the service members was required to wear the shrapnel-absorbing vests and helmets whenever they were outside. Whenever there was a danger of rocket or mortar attack – a constant threat – the vests were required inside buildings as well. The vests contained large ceramic plates that would stop small-caliber rounds from piercing a torso, but the protection was small consolation compared with the 30 pounds it added to their load as they walked around in the desert sun. Adding the weight of pistols, rifles, ammunition and the water they consumed constantly, every man and woman gained between 30 and 50 pounds from the time they crawled out of their sleeping bags to the time they stepped out the doors of their berthing areas. While the Marines couldn't control when a mortar or rocket would be fired at them, they could be prepared by wearing their protective gear.

Barclay stood and 'milled about smartly,' waiting for the meeting to begin. No one was ever late in the Marine Corps – fifteen minutes early was considered on time for this group of warriors. Barclay often chuckled as he thought of the monumental amount of time this would be if it was ever aggregated across the entire Marine Corps, but he saw the value in it – no one had to wait for anyone else to arrive, except the senior person leading the meeting. This senior-ranking officer was expected to roll in right on time.

The group wasn't disappointed. At exactly 9:00 a.m. local time, the tent flap opened and four men walked in. One of the men, shorter than the rest of the Marines in the room, stepped forward to call the meeting to order. He did not conform to the linebacker physique common among male Marines who were in the gym when not performing their duties. However, he commanded respect with a ramrod-straight spine and blue eyes that shone like gunmetal at the few dozen assembled Marines and coalition troops in the tent.

"For those of you who haven't had the displeasure of meeting me," the man said to the assembled Marines with a touch of humor, "my name is General Mathis, and you're here to plan a mission that I'll be on myself. One I likely won't be coming back from."

If Marines knew how to gasp, the group would have done so at that moment. General Mathis had survived combat in the Persian Gulf War and multiple tours in Afghanistan. He had led the charge for them just a year prior when they fought tooth-and-nail from Kuwait, across divisions of Iraqi Army regulars, and liberated Baghdad. Marines accepted they may have to sacrifice themselves or their troops on the orders of a leader like him – but him, sacrifice himself?

"I'll start with an overview of the situation here," Mathis said as he gestured toward the maps in the center of the room. "As you know, we've been dealing with a very active insurgency in the city of Fallujah for almost as long as we've been in Iraq. After failed negotiations with the tribal leaders over the last several months, we attempted to deliver medical supplies last week to a clinic in the northern part of the city and came under heavy attack."

The troops in the room nodded. Many of them had supported the patrol's evacuation and tended to the wounded when they arrived at the forward operating base they lived in.

"Obviously, if we can't engender goodwill and raise the quality of life for the Iraqi population, we don't have a purpose here. Earlier this week, we took some additional measures to get the tribal leaders' attention. We shut down water and power to the entire city." General Mathis paused for effect, and then added, "Not surprisingly, a day later we received a request from them to re-open negotiations."

Mathis continued by informing the group that the tribal leaders – the sheikhs – were only willing to negotiate with Mathis himself, accompanied by a small security detail. All other coalition forces had to pull back to the edge of the city or the patrol wouldn't be allowed past the heavily armed roadblocks. Any incursion by coalition forces anywhere in the city, and the ceasefire was off.

"I've seen too many missions to know that something isn't right about this," Mathis told the assembled Marines. "Our ground intelligence assets have informed me that there is a high likelihood they'll attempt to cut off our supporting units outside the city, ambush the patrol and take me hostage in order to gain some leverage. I told our folks – let's see them try. So as far as the tribal leaders are concerned, we're doing exactly what they're asking and sending a small patrol into the heart of the city center to meet with them."

Captain Barclay couldn't believe what he was hearing. The general was willingly going into a city of more than 300,000 people, most of them hostile to coalition forces, just to prove a point? The Marines and Army had spent the entire spring bombarding the city with artillery and searching house-to-house in order to clear neighborhoods of insurgents and weapons caches. As soon as their troops would leave a section of the city, insurgents would flow right back in like a dry sponge soaking up water. Learning from their failed efforts, the strategy was abandoned. Only heavily-armed patrols were allowed inside the city after that. No coalition unit had been to the city center in over a month, and even those troops didn't make it out unscathed.

"I know suicide missions aren't something we train for, but rest assured we will have every asset lined up outside the city to support us if need be," Mathis informed the group. "There are a lot of possible outcomes here. If they attempt to close off our route and ambush us, we'll finally have the excuse we need to do what we've been trying to do for over a year – secure this city for the civilian population. If they hold to their word and don't attack, we'll have the first chance we've ever had to meet these folks on their own ground and work out a ceasefire. Either way, its an opportunity too good to pass up."

Mathis paused for a moment and quickly scanned the room, checking each person with a quick look, much like a football coach sizing up his team before sending them to the field.

"Our mission objective is to send a lightly-armored patrol into the heart of Fallujah on June 15 to meet with the tribal council and return without being engaged by the enemy. If we are engaged either on our way in or out of the city, then Lord help them."

Barclay and the other Marines nodded – no one liked the odds, but their mission had just been given to them. It was now up to them to plan for the possible threats they would face and carry it out. Examining all the possible outcomes they might encounter was a benchmark of the planning process every officer learned – and one they came to rely on for their survival.

Mathis nodded to the task force intelligence officer who then stepped forward and addressed the group.

"We'll face the same risks we've been dealing with for months – highly-trained light infantry that are disguised among the civilian population," the intelligence officer said. He continued, "Mostly a threat from small arms, with a few machine guns and crew-served weapons here and there at choke points and major intersections."

He pointed down at the largest map on the table and touched the major intersections throughout the city.

"We've encountered plenty of rocket-propelled grenades capable of disabling our tanks and taking out our vehicles. Suicide bombers and improvised explosive devices are still a threat as we have an unknown amount of explosives and unexploded ordnance inside the city."

The intelligence officer paused, looked briefly at the general for confirmation, and then continued.

"A unique threat we're going to have to deal with here is the fact we have a very valuable target being sent, in effect, behind enemy lines. We have to consider the possibility that they will take the general hostage and plan accordingly for his extract."

The Marines nodded – they'd heard about these type of threats within Fallujah at every planning session they'd attended since taking command of the city the previous fall. An unknown factor was what they would do if their commander was captured. It wasn't a question of who would take his place. Similar to the President of the United States – affectionately referred to as 'POTUS' by the Marines – they knew who the next-senior person was, another general in Baghdad. However, the situation could turn into a public relations debacle if a captured Mathis were to be paraded through Fallujah and disgraced on a video that would be broadcast around the world. Such a thing would be an incredible blow to the morale of all the coalition forces in the country and in the Middle East. It would take a lot of resources to get him out if things went badly, and there was no guarantee they'd be able to get him out alive.

The intelligence officer gave the floor to the operations officer, a major with a barrel chest who began his brief on what resources the group would have available for the mission.

"Ladies and gents, because of the unique nature of this mission," the major said as he nodded in the general's direction, "we're pulling out all the stops for this one. We have a lot of possible changes we need to plan for. First, we'll need artillery staged and dialed into the city center. Anything to add from our artillery battery?"

The artillery battery commander, standing amongst the officers, shook his head back and forth in response, and the operations officer moved on.

"Next will be air support. In addition to fixed-wing drones monitoring the rooftops for snipers and a contingent of FA-18s, we'll need our Hueys providing close cover for the patrol. Captain Barclay, we good to go there?"

Barclay's spine straightened when he heard his name.

"Roger that, sir, we'll be good to go."

The operations officer continued, making sure the commanders of the medevac unit, sniper platoon, and infantry units all understood their involvement and added anything they thought would be helpful. Army special operators would be on call, in addition to a team of Navy SEALS, should a rescue team be needed for the general. Each of the sub-units had been training on how to deal with unexpected changes they might encounter on missions exactly like this.

"Now," said the operations officer, "we have the commander of the unit that's been tasked with patrolling Fallujah for the last few months, in addition to some folks who have had to fight their way out of ambushes in Fallujah and nearby Ramadi. They've encountered just about everything that could go wrong with a patrol in this city. Let's get their input on the things we need to know."

Each of the combat leaders stepped up and gave the group briefs on what they had encountered and how they responded when attacked at different locations and with different types of weapons. They also shared what they had entered into their after-action reports so future units would know what to do and what not to do if they experienced the same challenges inside Fallujah. While an outsider may think this kind of deep-dive would be overkill, the Marines knew their lives – and the lives of the men and women they commanded – were at stake. If they could learn about what to do or not do when faced with an unexpected risk, they were duty-bound to do so.

At this point in the planning session, the group split up into teams, ensuring there was someone from an air unit, a ground unit, and an artillery unit in each group. Each taking a corner of the tent, the groups set about planning what they could only call a very strange mission. The best-case scenario was that the patrol would come under heavy attack as it traversed the main highway running into the center of the town. In that case, they would simply turn around and escape. It was more likely Mathis would make it into the meeting and then be taken hostage. However, their mission objective was not to plan for what would most likely happen – they had to plan for what they wanted their outcome to be. Each of them had participated in this process a dozen times. They understood that by harnessing the collective experience of the group, more often than not they were able to plan for success in situations that at first seemed impossible.

Captain Barclay was leading his small team, so he began:

"Alright, I guess the most obvious place to start with this would be staging our support units. Where are we going to place our artillery, and when?"

Barclay worked with his artillery representative, a gunnery sergeant who had spent his entire adult life in an artillery battery, to decide where the Howitzer cannons – 16,000 pound weapons that had to be transported on the back of what amounted to a semi-truck trailer – would be positioned. The 155mm rounds they fired could travel for miles and accurately hit a single building. Using them in an urban environment brought with it some challenges, however. First, the high-explosive rounds didn't discriminate between enemy and civilian – the Marines had to be very careful where they fired so as not to hit civilians. Second, the Marines who manned the weapons were targets for enemy snipers – to stage them within striking distance of the city center put them at risk of enemy attack from the tall buildings on the edge of the city. Barclay and the gunnery sergeant, along with the executive officer of an infantry battalion, planned how they would stage the cannons and where the best natural cover would be outside the city.

The artillery representative had encountered a lot of last-minute changes in his career. Whether it was dialing in his weapons in a sandstorm or repairing a broken Howitzer in the middle of a fire mission, he had solved hundreds of problems. Any one of these problems, the group knew, might be encountered on this mission. With the general's life at stake, there wasn't room for error. The changes they were most likely to face were accounted for and built into their plan.

Next, the group planned for the infantry troops that would be needed on-call in case the general was captured or the patrol was attacked. A small special operations force could attempt an extraction. However, the rest of the patrol would be trapped in a hornet's nest of highly-trained fighters who would be heavily rewarded for every coalition troop they took hostage or killed. The infantry troops suffered from the same problem as the artillery Marines did – if they were close enough to offer support within minutes, they were vulnerable to enemy sniper fire and mortar attack. Therefore, they would need to stage their vehicles outside the range of both threats, increasing the time it would take to respond if called. Barclay, the artillery gunnery sergeant and the infantry battalion's executive officer pored over the map of the city. The group assessed the route the patrol would likely need to take and planned where to stage the infantry's mounted platoons so they could get past any potential roadblocks the insurgents might set up.

All the what-ifs, the unknown risks and possible changes were making Barclay's head spin. What if the patrol was attacked on the way in? On the way out? What if insurgents blocked the main supply route into the city, stopping the mounted infantry units from providing help? What if the artillery battery was attacked by sniper fire, drawing corpsmen away from the field hospital and making them unavailable to help the Marines in the patrol?

Fortunately, Barclay had experienced this feeling before and knew how to handle it. He looked around the tent and saw three other groups doing the same thing his was doing – creating a detailed plan that accounted for the changes they each had experienced in the past. Each of the groups would come together in a few minutes and present their individual plans. The best tactics would be combined into the final plan. Then, that plan would be used to train the Marines stepping out on the patrol and those who would be providing support by land and air. Knowing there was a process behind his team's efforts calmed him enough to get all his team's ideas down on paper.

Now it was his turn to plan how the air assets – both fixed wing aircraft and those with rotors – would be used. All the planes were staged at an airfield well outside the city, but each of the aircraft could be at Fallujah within minutes. While the intelligence-gathering drones would be flying a thousand feet above the city, his helicopter squadron would be just a few hundred feet above the buildings. That distance allowed them to provide close air support to the patrol and the troops staged on the outskirts of the city. Additionally, the FA-18s would be thousands of feet in the air, keeping watch and ready to be called into action with precision strikes if needed.

Finally, the group was done factoring in the most likely changes they would encounter and recording the steps they thought best for the mission. Barclay gathered his folks along the side of the tent and waited as the other teams finished.

When all the teams were done creating their plans, Mathis called in other officers from air, ground and artillery units, as well as some Iraqi Army officers that were raised in Fallujah and knew the city's layout. These men sat around the table in the center of room and faced the first group as they presented their draft of the plan.

One by one, each of the teams presented their plan to the assembled group. One by one, each team's plan was picked apart. Had they considered that a dust storm could eliminate visibility for all the aircraft and drones, eliminating the capability to provide close air support? Had they considered that motorcycles were being used to attack coalition forces and this allowed insurgents to cross through roadblocks that would stop Humvees? While the teams had brought their collective knowledge of the changes they had encountered in their careers, it was vital to get a second opinion. The additional viewpoints each brought another set of experiences in the likely changes they would encounter.

At the end of the session with the new team members, each of the planning teams had lines drawn through parts of their plan. The lines represented instances where they learned something they hadn't considered, rendering an idea useless or ineffective. The operations officer and intelligence officer then combined the best parts of the separate plans.

At the end, they had a solid plan that gave them all hope they just might be able to get the general in and out of the city without being attacked. And if they were attacked, that had hope that they would be able to extract the patrol with a minimum number of casualties. But the planning session wasn't done.

"Well folks, we still need to consider a big 'what if' here – and that's what if they do what we think they want to do and try to capture me in that meeting?" Mathis asked the group. With a few more suggestions from the teams, they had built a solid contingency plan to extract the general and then get the patrol out of the city. While they couldn't factor in every possible change they would face, they all felt they had definitely prepared for the most likely ones. Experience taught them that trying to come up with a plan to deal with change in the middle of combat never yielded optimal results. Therefore, they planned for change before the change occurred.

The only thing left to do was to name the mission before they brought it back to their teams. Mathis informed them he already had a name in mind. It would be on the request for support documents and mission forms the operations officer sent out prior to all of them stepping off in just a few days.

With a wave of Mathis' hand, the room was called to attention.

"Good work, Marines. Now it's time to get your people ready," Mathis announced.

One of the officers called, "Atten-tion!" Mathis turned, followed by the men he had entered the tent with, and the leadership team exited.

Once the general was gone, someone called, "Carry On!" and the group relaxed.

Barclay turned and grabbed his flak jacket and helmet from the pile on the ground. They were now cold from the combination of cooled sweat and the air conditioner still chugging away along the wall. He buckled his chinstrap, put on his sunglasses and moved back out into the light, the heat hitting him like stepping into an open oven.

A week later Barclay was in the cockpit of his Huey, running his pre-flight checklist. He'd gotten word over the radio that the patrol of 15 vehicles had just left Camp Fallujah and was on its way to the city center. After clearing his takeoff with the tent that served as their air traffic control tower, he took one more look at his flight path before lifting the control stick of his helicopter. This motion sent a wash of dust and sand into the air around him. As his squadron of Hueys lifted into the air and headed toward the wall of buildings in the distance that made up the edge of Fallujah, Barclay couldn't help but laugh at Mathis' humor. On the top of his checklist was written the name Mathis had chosen for the mission: Dead Man's Patrol.

"Whatever happens," Barclay thought, "this is going to be a day to remember."

THE BUSINESS: PLAN, PART II

April 1, 2014
Los Angeles, CA

Raymond Barclay looked out over the cityscape that stretched before him. The windows in his office were tinted to protect the room from the sun, but as he often reminded himself, "It'll never get to be 117 degrees in here, so it always feels like the air conditioning is on."

His office was spartan in comparison to those of his peers. He had a single picture of his wife and 9-year-old daughter on his desk and some framed pictures on the walls. Everything else was as neat and tidy as his old office at Cherry Point, NC. It had been an interesting ten years since he took off from the air base in Iraq to provide overwatch for Mathis' patrol. One picture on the wall across from his desk looked back at him. It was Barclay and his three crew members from that patrol – his co-pilot and two door gunners – all in their flight suits and posed next to the Huey before takeoff. All of them had made it home from that deployment by the skin of their teeth. Since then, each had gone their separate ways. Barclay had exited the Marine Corps and gone back to school for his MBA. Although it was fun, the thought of continuing to fly helicopters didn't appeal to him or his young wife.

After some internships, he had found himself working as a mid-level manager in one of the top athletic clothing brands in the country. Professional athletes were lining up to be paid to wear the shoes and clothing his company produced. Although Barclay kept himself away from the marketing side of the organization, it was still fun to see the superstars occasionally walking the halls of their office going to and from sponsorship negotiations. That spring, Barclay had been promoted to vice president of strategic development for the company. His supervisors had noticed that Barclay had a very unique planning process that he used on the smaller projects he had been in charge of. Even when things changed at the last minute, Barclay's teams always managed to reach their goals. Although Barclay attributed their success to the hard work and wisdom of his peers, leadership in his company saw that he had a mind for innovating solutions. It was a skill they would need in order to make up lost revenue from a lagging year and an upcoming product launch they hoped would bring them back from being in the red.

Barclay checked his watch and saw that he was 15 minutes away from leading his first strategic planning session for the vice presidents and CEO of the multi-billion-dollar company he worked for. This would be his chance to show them they had made the right decision in promoting him. It was also his chance to shape strategy for the organization, its employees and for the athletic clothing market in general. He had spent hours researching the best practices of his competitors, market trends and the financials of his own company before a familiar feeling swept over him – that it was too much information for a single person to take in. He decided to go with what had made him successful in his military career – leveraging the wisdom of the planning group to achieve their objectives. His planning method was something these senior leaders had never seen, but Barclay knew it worked in changing environments and in reaching challenging objectives. It would work here as well.

He walked down the hall to the meeting room, greeting his fellow vice presidents along the way. The men and women filed into a boardroom that had an even better view of the city outside. The tall buildings stretched out all around them, rising like stairs on the valley's hills before the land became too steep to support them. Barclay lowered the blinds so the group could work without being blinded by the midday sun. He had already set up the boards he would need in the room. The center of the conference table was bare of maps, but it did have a stack of legal pads arranged on it.

Their CEO, a short, round man with sharp eyes and an always-ready smile, stepped into the room and took his place at the head of the table. He began:

"Alright team, we're here because, honestly, we failed last year."

Each member of the team nodded – despite their best efforts, the company reached only 70% of its financial goals on their last product launch. Fortunately, the company had a 30-year track record of growth, so one lagging year wasn't enough to make their shareholders jump ship. However, there was plenty of speculation that their successful run was coming to an end.

Their CEO continued, "Our job here today is to figure out how to turn that around. We considered bringing in consultants who have helped us do trend analysis in the past, but a member of our team," the CEO glanced at Barclay, "convinced me that maybe another approach would get us better results. We've all cleared our calendars for the next few hours, so I expect no one to be taking calls or taking extended breaks. This plan is our priority."

With this, the CEO nodded at Barclay, turning the meeting over to him. Barclay stood and moved to the back wall of the boardroom, toward the empty boards he had staged there the night before.

"We know we took a hit last year with a failed launch," Barclay began, "but we don't have to again. As you'll recall, we took a hard look at what our competition was doing in the same athletic apparel space and built a plan to beat them at their own game. Unfortunately, we were plagued by changes we never saw coming - supply-chain hold-ups and a view that we were a commodity retailers could shuffle around on their shelves."

The members of the group nodded once again. They had read the industry reports of retailers moving their newest product around the store in an attempt to keep up with the lowest-priced apparel. It was a change they hadn't planned for and not one they wanted to be unprepared for again.

"Instead of looking at what our competition was doing and building a plan to counter it, I thought we'd try something different. Something that would allow us to get ahead with our next launch and seize the initiative," Barclay told the group.

The CEO's familiar smile came back – seizing the initiative was what had allowed the brand to stay relevant and profitable in the past. He had spent a lot of money bringing in industry experts to teach him and his team about innovation, but those same experts were teaching his competitors too. He needed another strategy and hoped he would find it in his new VP.

Barclay continued, "I strongly believe that all the information we need to be successful with our next launch can be found right here in this company, specifically with the leaders in this room. Each of you has faced these challenges before, either here or in other positions you've held. What we need to do is get that information out of your heads and into a detailed action plan for our departments."

He walked to the blank board on the left side of the room and wrote two words: Business Objective.

"While those words may make sense to the folks in here, let me explain what they mean in the context of this meeting," Barclay said. "An objective has to be three things – precise, profitable and in line with our purpose. If you'll recall, last year's mission objective, or our version of it, was to dominate the athletic apparel industry and gain 20% more market share than our competitors with our new product. While that goal was, and is, fully achievable, it wasn't precise enough for us to act on within each of our departments. Going through the after-action meetings I did with each department head when I stepped into my position, I discovered that each of us was executing at a very high rate but that our actions weren't aligned toward a precise and profitable goal."

It pained some of the team members to hear this, but no one could argue. Each of their departments had performed spectacularly. Marketing had the company's advertisements in all the popular sports magazines – almost twice as many as their competitors. Operations had cut costs of production in their international facilities, creating excess capital to reinvest. And the distribution network had expanded their line into retailers that had previously avoided athletic apparel. None of the vice presidents had received poor performance reports, and yet the company had still dipped in profitability. The launch was lambasted in industry journals that picked apart the supply-chain holdups and mistakes they'd made with top retailers in guaranteeing prominent product placement. Each of them had to admit they worked hard the prior year, but were pulling on opposite ends of the rope.

"This afternoon, I'm going to walk us through a process to build a strategy that will allow us to innovate some new solutions for our next launch, stay a step ahead of the changes we encountered last year and reach our goal of gaining 20% of our competitor's market share. Sound good?" Barclay asked the assembled leaders.

Heads around the room nodded. They knew they had to do something different if they were going to bring their shareholder value back to the performance investors had become used to.

Barclay began by saying, "Let's start with our objective. We know we want to capture 20% of our competitor's market share with our upcoming launch, but how do we measure 'dominate the athletic apparel industry'?"

"Well," another vice president ventured, "it means that our product is getting prime shelf space at our retailers."

"That's good, but I think Barclay is pointing at something more," the CEO added. "Prime shelf space won't guarantee that people are buying our products, and great display space doesn't always equate to sales."

"Right," said Barclay. "So we need to look at hard metrics. What will show us, unequivocally, that we have dominated the athletic apparel industry with our next product in a way that benefits our shareholders?"

"That's easy," said the chief financial officer, who thus far had been silent. "If we can cap three billion in overall sales throughout the company, we'll be doing better than our next two competitors combined. The launch will be a major boost toward that goal."

"Great," Barclay said. He turned to the CFO and asked, "And what is our new product line projected to achieve by the end of next year's Q4?"

"Two-hundred and fifty million by the end of next year," the CFO replied. "That may be a stretch because our last product launch only hit half of its projected number, so maybe we should lower our goal … "

The CEO was about to cut in when Barclay said, "I believe that 250 million is an achievable goal, and that with a shared process, we will be able to reach it."

Barclay turned to the board behind him and wrote '250 million in new product sales by end of Q4.' "What else?" he asked the group.

"Well, 250 million in new sales is an awesome goal, but we want to make sure that people are buying our products instead of our competitors', now and in the future," said another vice president. "What if we shoot for 250 million in sales and a certain percentage of more shelf and advertising space? That will get us our financial goal and allow us to hit our growth metrics."

"If we could gain 40% more advertising space and increase our distribution channels by 15%, we'd be there," the chief marketing officer added.

"Good," Barclay said as he captured the idea on the board. "So what I have for a mission objective is '250 million in new product sales, 40% more advertising space and an increase of distribution channels by 15% by the end of Q4.' Is that a precise goal that will make us profitable, get us on track, and combined with other sales, lead us to 3 billion in overall revenue?"

Every head around the table nodded.

"Are we really trying to get that done by the end of Q4?" one vice president inquired. "This objective could take us five years to accomplish."

"That's true," Barclay agreed, "but without a date we can't build backwards and create a timeline. Additionally, having a deadline moves everyone toward a common goal and gives us a goal when we encounter change."

The meeting was going better than he had initially planned, but Barclay knew there was more work to do.

"Because this mission has multiple individual goals, it can really be broken up into multiple sub-missions that we can all pursue together. For the sake of today's session, let's get enough planned so that I can get with each of the sub-teams and work with them to build out their individual mission plans next week," Barclay said.

"Next," he continued, "we need to look at the risks involved with this mission objective. In other words, what could stand in our way of accomplishing this? What changes did we face last time and what changes are we likely to face this year?"

"Well, for one, the Olympics are ramping up and the distribution channels are going to become flooded with athletic apparel. That also means marketing space for our apparel will be going for a premium," the CMO said.

"Those are all valid points," Barclay responded, "and we'll capture them. But what I want to do is have everyone take one of these legal pads and write down potential risks in clear enough language that they don't take up more than one line. Do that on your own, and then we'll combine the lists and cross out duplicates."

While the leaders set to work listing out all the risks, Barclay prepared for the next part of the planning process. It would be the same one he had seen countless times in military planning sessions – lining up resources.

"Ok, as you get done listing your risks, tear off that sheet and pass it over to our scribe," Barclay said as he looked over at his administrative assistant who had joined them in the meeting. "My assistant Jan will begin compiling them while we work on resources."

After making her way around the table to gather the sheets, Jan began laying them out in front of her and going through the lists. She crossed out obvious duplicates before compiling the rest on a blank sheet. Finally, she began to transfer that sheet to one of the boards along the wall.

"As you can see, we have quite a few changes to account for as we set out to accomplish this mission objective," Barclay told the group. "What I want us to do now is look at the ones that we can affect – for instance, changes in our distribution network – and the ones we can't affect – like another recession."

The group went through each of the risks and figured out which ones they could affect and which ones were outside their control, just as Barclay had done when planning in the military. Instead of highly trained enemy troops and weapons systems, he was looking at economic and supply-chain factors, but the process was the same.

"As you look at all these risks, I want you to each think of the resources that we may be able to leverage to handle these changes – the leadership, systems, technology, relationships with outside vendors – anything you can imagine that could deal with things that tripped us up last time or could get in our way in the coming year," Barclay instructed. "Do the same thing and list those on a sheet of paper."

The group members each looked at the list of risks that Jan posted on the white board and began brainstorming everything they could think of that would handle them. Again, they tore off their sheets and passed them to Jan who compiled the lists and wrote the resources on the next board.

"Rarely have we looked at what changes to our plan we'll face before we launch and figure out what resources we have available to mitigate them. But we're missing a major resource, and perhaps the most valuable one," Barclay told the group. "Who participated in last year's product launch?"

Half of the hands in the room rose.

"Please keep your hands up. Now," continued Barclay, "who has participated in a product launch of any kind in their careers?"

The rest of the hands in the room went up.

"Great! Each of you knows something that will help us make this next launch successful. I want you to write all of your ideas for how to make things better this year on the next sheet of paper and pass them to Jan," Barclay told the group.

The team members spent a longer time on this part of the planning session. For some of them, this task meant reaching back into what was multiple decades of experience dealing with product launches in multiple industries.

Jan compiled these lessons and posted them on the next whiteboard.

"At this point, it's time to build our strategy for this next product launch," Barclay said. "What I'd like each of us to do is break up into teams. There should be at least one person from operations, one person from marketing, and one person from sales on each team. If you need to grab someone else from the building you can, just make sure they have experience dealing with the changes we've encountered in the past or are likely to encounter this year. Look at the boards if you need a reminder."

"This session is a priority," the CEO reminded the group. "Whatever your folks are doing, this is more important."

Some team members scuttled out of the room to grab more members from their departments, while others began forming groups. Ten minutes later, four groups had formed and were building individual plans for the company's product launch, frequently glancing at the board of risks, resources and lessons. An hour later, each team had built a step-by-step plan for how they would achieve the mission objective.

"Now, let's get our folks from legal, the distribution channel supervisors, and our media department to have a look at the plans," Barclay said.

The crew of examiners were waiting outside the board room door when Barclay opened it, and they shuffled in and sat at the board room table. One by one, each of the groups presented their plan. The examiners asked questions about legal ramifications of manufacturing decisions, how the supply chain would support increasing distribution, and whether they could secure the athletes the groups asked to represent the new product line. Each of the questions addressed an unforeseen change that cost the company revenue last year, or unexpected changes they had seen throughout their careers. Once each of the four groups' plans were presented, the examiners left the room and the groups were allowed to incorporate their feedback, rearrange their plans or scrap entire pieces of it if necessary.

"Now that we all have solid outlines, let's combine them into a single, cohesive plan," Barclay said. He used one of the boards to list out the action steps each of the four groups came up with, eliminating duplicates and refining the ones where clarity was needed. Each of the action steps looked like mission objectives of their own, including a person responsible for completing it:

- Secure three new manufacturing facilities to produce the product by the end of Q1 – Chief of Operations

- Sign five All-American and professional-level athletes to support product launch by end of Q2 – VP of Media Relations

- Expand distribution fleet by 30% to accommodate increased distribution channels by end of Q2 – VP of Manufacturing

Barclay continued writing action items on the board until they numbered more than twenty. When he finished he turned to his CEO and asked if there was anything to add to the action items.

"That's a helluva plan. It's definitely more detail than we've had in the past," the CEO said to Barclay and the assembled leaders.

"But we're not done yet, sir," Barclay said. "Remember that we listed a few possible changes that were out of our control earlier – we need to factor those in and make sure we have an action plan if they occur."

The group then went through the uncontrollable changes they identified earlier. If the economy swung down again, how would they know and what would they do? If they couldn't sign the latest star athletes, which ones would they target next and what deadline would force them to act?

Once the last step was complete, Barclay stepped to the center of the room and addressed the group:

"We've done some great work here today. Instead of scrambling to deal with all our foreseeable problems as they arise, we've set up ways to deal with them beforehand. For those of you whose name is tied to one of these action steps," Barclay motioned toward the final mission plan written on the wall's whiteboard, "what I'd like each of you to do is find some time in your calendars next week. You and I will get together with your teams and run a similar mission planning process. That way we can make sure we each stay on track toward meeting our shared mission objective. It won't take too long, and you'll be facilitating the majority of it from what you learned here today. Jan has my availabilities and can make sure each of your teams gets on my calendar."

The members of the team filed out of the board room and back to their offices. They had something none of them had since stepping into leadership positions at the company – a precise goal each of them shared a part of and owned together. They had come up with creative ways to advertise their new product and get it to market while accounting for the most likely changes to the plan they would encounter.

Barclay stayed behind in the boardroom after the CEO shook his hand and left. Jan gathered the papers from the wall and went back to their shared office to start scheduling the mission planning sessions Barclay would be leading next week. It had been a full day, and a lot had been accomplished. Barclay stood and walked toward the windows overlooking the cityscape around him. He re-opened the blinds and let his eyes adjust to the late afternoon light reflecting from the glass panels on the buildings around him.

He thought to himself, "We've made a plan, but my work's only just begun."

PREPARE

Photo By Author, Iraq 2004

THE MISSION: PREPARE, PART I

June 13, 2004
South Compound, Camp Fallujah, Iraq

As Staff Sgt. Fulton stepped out of his company's headquarters tent and began walking toward the row of parked vehicles, he looked out at the Marines who had been waiting since before the sun came up. Some were in the driver and passenger seats of the green and tan Humvees. Others were sitting in the large truck beds that made up the rear of the vehicles. A few others stood behind the large mounted weapons that were alternately angled out and resting on their bases. Machine guns and automatic grenade launchers were standard fare for most patrols, but Fulton wondered if they would be enough for the one they were about to embark on. Although he was aware of the work that went into the planning of this mission, he knew firsthand of all the changes that could occur. However, his leadership hadn't let him down before and he was confident they wouldn't today either.

For the last five days, the two squads of Marines had been practicing vehicle maneuvers in the large, empty lot that made up the south end of Camp Fallujah. They practiced for every conceivable change their patrol's plan may encounter – the lead vehicle being disabled by a roadside bomb, the patrol being separated by an ambush, the rear vehicle being cut off from the rest of the patrol. In any situation, Fulton felt confident that his Marines would know what to do. They had been deployed together for four months, running combat operations all over the Sunni Triangle, the geographic area within Iraq with points at Baghdad, Fallujah and Ramadi. They'd seen plenty of action, even losing a few men who were medically evacuated to Germany and then to hospitals in the United States. When Fulton learned of their next mission and its title, Dead Man's Patrol, he wondered if he might soon be adding to the number of letters he would be writing home to his Marines' families.

While the dozens of Marines in the vehicles knew they were being prepared for a special mission, they didn't know the exact details of every unit involved. It was policy to not disclose anything that may tip off the enemy. If one of the Marines mentioned something in an email or a phone call home, the entire operation could be compromised. Fulton himself had learned the exact purpose of the patrol only a few hours before and was trying to figure out the best way to break it to the Marines. He wanted them to understand the gravity of the situation but didn't want to shake their confidence.

As a platoon sergeant, Fulton was in charge of the lives and welfare of 30 Marines. He was their father, their boss, and their big brother while they were deployed. Fulton reported to the platoon commander, who in turn reported to the company commander, who reported to the battalion commander, who reported directly to General Mathis. Although there were three people between him and the general, it was General Mathis himself who had stopped by the company tent to meet Fulton and make sure everything was squared away with his Marines. After multiple combat deployments to Iraq and Afghanistan, there were only two events that made Fulton nervous – when they served lobster and steak in the chow hall and when the 'brass' came down to visit troops before a mission. Either of those events meant that the Marines were going to be ordered to do something that any sane individual would refuse outright. When the Marines lined up for chow the previous night, they were served steaks and lobsters (no one bothered to ask how the lobster had come to reach them in the desert a few thousand miles away from where it was caught – probably because they didn't want to know the answer). That event made Fulton worry a little. When he walked into the company tent that morning and saw General Mathis, his battalion commander, company commander and platoon commander standing around a desk, his heart sank. Whatever it was they were going to ask of him and his Marines, it was going to be difficult. They gave him the details of the patrol's mission – ingress and egress routes, timelines and contingency plans for the most likely changes they would encounter and told him they'd be stepping off in an hour.

Fulton put his personal feelings aside as he approached the Marines waiting in their vehicles. No matter what he thought about the mission, he couldn't let his emotions affect their performance. If they saw their leader in a nervous state, it could destroy troop morale and affect their ability to perform. Fulton knew they would need every bit of skill they could muster if they were going to survive the day. He put his arm in the air and moved his hand in a wide circle, signaling to the Marines to leave their vehicles and circle up around him. It was time to prepare.

The Marines grabbed their personal weapons – rifles, pistols, and shotguns – and hopped down from their vehicles to gather in a semicircle around Fulton. Fulton always felt a bit like a teacher, as most of the Marines were barely out of high school. The Marines trotted toward him, each wearing the flak jacket, helmet and protective gear required. The Marines knew what to expect in this meeting – they'd been through countless pre-mission briefs in training and on deployment. The non-commissioned officers among them stood ready with notepads, the junior Marines stood ready and listened. They knew they weren't about to participate in a meeting where back-and-forth conversation would occur. These briefs were short, sweet and to the point. The only questions asked were clarifying ones. Each of them knew the mission they were about to run had been planned to the smallest detail. They also knew the details were so complex that there wasn't time for a single person to take all of it in. Their patrol only needed to know the overall objective and any changes likely to affect their specific part of the mission. Fulton took a deep breath, and began:

"Listen up, Marines. Get your watches out for a time hack. It will be zero-seven-one-zero in 5 ... 4 ... 3 ... 2 ... 1 ... and hack."

The Marines in the platoon set their digital watches to Fulton's. They each knew that timelines on missions were coordinated down to the second. They realized they would likely be working with multiple support units who all needed to be operating from the same clock.

"As you know, over the last several weeks we've been trying to get the support of the tribal leaders that control Fallujah's militias," Fulton told the group of Marines. "And we've been largely unsuccessful. A few days ago, our engineers shut off the city's water supply and electricity in the hopes of forcing their leaders to agree to a ceasefire and begin negotiating. Our tactics got their attention."

The Marines chuckled at this statement. Many of them had been on deployments where they had to live without electricity. And due to the speed at which they moved when securing regions of Iraq and Afghanistan, they often had to go days without a resupply of water. They knew how vital these things were to maintaining a basic quality of life.

"The sheikhs, the tribal leaders in the city, agreed to call a ceasefire and negotiate with us to have their water and electricity turned back on, but on one condition – that General Mathis be sent in to handle the negotiations."

General Mathis was a legend among the Marines. He had a reputation for valuing the lives of the troops who served him and was not afraid to use the weapons he had available to keep them safe. Not to mention, that to an enlisted Marine, a general held a place of respect just above Jesus and just below the Almighty Himself.

"So," began Fulton, "your mission objective is to safely transport General Mathis and two Marine translators from Camp Fallujah to the city center along the main eastern supply route and get them back safely. You'll depart at zero-eight-hundred and return when the general is ready for egress, which we are planning to occur at twelve-hundred."

The Marines nodded, the ones with notebooks recording the timeline and details. They waited to be told what supporting units would be following them in. What armored tanks or troop carriers would be providing cover as they entered and exited the city.

"If all goes well, your patrol will be the only one entering and leaving the city today," Fulton added.

The steely confidence of the younger Marines wavered at this statement. They had all been on patrols in Fallujah and affectionately referred to it as the 'Wild West.' Any coalition unit that entered the city limits was guaranteed to be engaged by rockets, small arms fire, improvised explosive devices – or a combination of all of them. As a result, it had become policy to not enter without heavy armored support. The preferred support was a tank that weighed as much as nine elephants and was made out of a metal so hard its exact composition was classified (though it was rumored to contain depleted uranium). To hear their small group of Humvees would be the only ones going into the city meant they would be sitting ducks for the 300,000 citizens they'd been tangling with for months. Not to mention the high-value target they were transporting would be a trophy their enemies would be proud to claim. If Mathis' face ended up on Al-Jazeera television as a hostage, the Marine Corps would level the city to get him back, meaning more of their fellow Marines wouldn't be returning home.

"Obviously, the enemy knows we're coming," Fulton said. "We can assume they will uphold the ceasefire, which means we can hope the small arms, mortar and rocket fire we've encountered won't be a problem today. Our greatest risks will be our own weapons – we're going in locked and loaded but can't afford an accidental discharge. It could literally be the spark that sets off a powder keg. All weapons will be kept loaded and on safe unless you are directly engaged. Random potshots at the patrol will not be a reason to return fire."

The Marines understood the change in their rules of engagement, but weren't happy with it. They had each spent hundreds of hours training to use their weapons, and the thought of someone being able to fire at them without the ability to return fire didn't sit well with them. The Marines were famous for their marksmanship. and each of them was trained to fire accurately from moving vehicles during the day, night and even in sandstorms. Being shot at without the ability to fire back was not something they were comfortable with.

"Because of the unique nature of our cargo, we will have every supporting unit in a fifty kilometer radius staged outside the city to provide cover and extraction capabilities if needed," Fulton told the assembled group. "Stand by to record the radio channel for both air and artillery support …"

Fulton read the radio channels the forward air controllers would be on aloud to the Marines. Additionally, he gave them the channel for the artillery battery staged outside the city. If the situation required it, the Marines would need to be able to communicate with the other teams and read grid coordinates for targets. Even the lowest-ranking Marine was trained in how to call in air support and targets for fire missions. During their training, their instructors shared stories of Marines in the world wars, Vietnam and Korea whose units were so decimated that it was up to a private or private-first-class to call for supporting fire to save their entire unit. These stories were legends in their world.

"Mathis will be in the second vehicle, along with one of his translators," Fulton continued. "The second translator will be in the third vehicle. Marines who would normally take those seats will shift to the rear of their vehicles to provide security."

Though the Marines were most comfortable in their regular positions, they were also trained to be proficient in any of the five or more positions within their vehicles. It was not uncommon for a Marine in a position to be injured, requiring another Marine to take his place. It was one of the many changes they were prepared for.

"When we arrive at the city center, you will use your normal vehicle spacing, dismount, and stay close to the vehicles to provide security to the compound. We won't have access to the rear of the building that General Mathis will enter, and we don't want to give the impression that we're surrounding it. The locals might get antsy at that. Keep your radios on, and when he's ready to depart, we'll mount the Humvees and egress along our same route of ingress," Fulton said.

The mission didn't leave a lot of room for error – if something happened to the general inside the building, he'd only have two translators for protection. And the Marines knew how quickly someone could disappear within the maze of alleys in the city. With an inability to surround the building – as well as not being able to communicate with the Marines in the building – they wouldn't know if the general had been taken hostage until he was already gone. Even a single point of failure was something the Marines were uncomfortable with – now they were dealing with multiple potential changes that were all outside their control.

"On the off-chance that we are engaged on our way into the city, we will use our normal protocol of egress and abandon the mission objective," Fulton said. "If they don't keep their word for the ceasefire, they'll have to burn candles for a few more days."

The Marines had practiced – and participated – in this emergency maneuver many times when on mounted patrol. It involved engaging the enemy while all the vehicles quickly turned around and retreated; one of the many changes to their mission's plan they were prepared for.

"If we are engaged while Mathis is inside the building with the tribal leaders, one squad will enter the building and secure the general while the other forms a perimeter around all sides of the building," Fulton told the Marines. "We will extract the general and egress along the main supply route we entered on. In the case of us being engaged while exiting the city, we will fire through the threat and get out, no sticking around to eliminate anything. Getting the general out is our primary objective – not eliminating the threat."

Fulton had yet to cover the change the Marines feared the most. It was also the most likely one – that their exit route would be blocked and they would be trapped inside the city.

"On the off-chance our enemy is stupid enough to stop us from leaving the city, we head for the closest of the four safe houses we've identified along the main supply route and call in for air and artillery support," Fulton said. "We've chosen these houses for their high walls and enclosed courtyards. We should be able to secure the perimeter and rooftops of these buildings. A special operations unit is on standby to extract the general. The rest of us will sit tight until we can fight our way out or get supporting units in to evacuate us."

The Marines nodded.

"Any clarifications needed?" Fulton asked.

The Marines remained silent.

"Very well. We step off in …" Fulton checked his watch, "40 minutes. Prep your vehicles, check your ammo and make sure you have everything you need to get through the night in case we end up staying late for the party."

The Marines walked back to their vehicles and began running through their pre-patrol checklist, the same one they'd done when they arrived at their vehicles an hour and a half prior. They re-checked their supplies of ammunition, water and food. Squad leaders re-checked their vehicle's fuel levels and ensured their extra fuel containers were topped off. Although the patrol was not scheduled to take more than an hour, the Marines had learned through experience that things could change in an instant and they may be stuck in a city overnight. It was better to have a piece of gear – like night vision goggles – and not need it, than to need it and find it unavailable.

At 7:55, General Mathis and his two translators walked from the company tent and loaded into the vehicles that were already running and radiating heat in the morning sun that crested the flat horizon. After a final radio check, the 15 vehicles began crawling forward until they exited the gate in the wall of the compound that they called Camp Fallujah.

Staff Sgt. Fulton, riding in the second-to-last vehicle, was confident that his Marines had all the information they would need to make this a successful mission, no matter what changes they encountered. As the vehicle left the relative safety of the compound and began travelling along the blacktop road, the tires began rumbling, reminding him of the roar of a crowd of people. The sound brought up old memories in Fulton's mind. When he was a child, his parents had taken him to see his first circus. He had watched in awe as a man, armed only with a bullwhip, put his head inside the jaws of an enormous lion. When the lion's teeth began closing around the lion tamer's head, Fulton remembered hiding his face in his small hands.

As the buildings on the outskirts of Fallujah grew closer, Fulton knew how that lion tamer must have felt.

THE BUSINESS: PREPARE PART 2

November 8, 2015
Chicago, IL

Tim Fulton waited patiently as the chain-link fence retracted in front of his pickup truck, allowing him into the parking lot. He edged the truck forward, waving at the security guard in his glass hut. It was a clear day, and he was excited to be driving into the parking lot of the printing company he had been working for during the last five years. Starting as a technician, Fulton had worked his way up the ranks to become a shift supervisor. The company ran three shifts each day, turning out large-format products for advertisers and companies all over the nation. For a company that operated their presses 24 hours a day, they had done well in keeping their equipment maintained and their business profitable.

Fulton could humbly claim that he had contributed to their success. As a senior technician, he had witnessed one of their three printing machines break down, stopping the entire production line as everyone from all three machines stood around and attempted to fix the downed machine. Although a broken machine wasn't unheard of for the employees, it was a significant enough change to disrupt their entire shift. Through interviews and studying in his off-time, Fulton learned what he needed to in order to establish a maintenance schedule and implement it, cutting the downtime of the printing machines considerably. Of course, they would still jam or break occasionally. After speaking with his shift supervisor, he worked out a protocol for when any of the machines went down. Instead of everyone milling around the broken machine, the team working with the malfunctioning printing press would shift their work over to one of the functioning machines and continue production while a trained member of the team worked to get the broken machine back online. When the protocol was followed, production remained steady, thereby increasing overall production compared to what it had been when all work stopped for a broken machine. Fulton's shift supervisor was awarded for the increased production with a promotion, creating a vacancy for a shift supervisor, and Fulton was ideally positioned to step into the role.

Grabbing his coffee from his truck's cup holder, Fulton locked his truck's door and walked into the large warehouse that housed the three presses, administrative offices and a design department. Greeting the administrative assistants on his way in, he stored his gear in a locker and stepped out onto the warehouse floor where the last shift was wrapping up their work.

Fulton checked in with the shift supervisor he would be relieving and learned that one of the machines had gone down after an hour of use during the previous shift. However, they had used the protocol Fulton developed and were able to get most of their orders loaded onto the delivery trucks and out the door. There was some leftover work they hadn't been able to finish due to the downed machine, but all three machines were up and running again. As a result, Fulton's shift was expected to make up the lost time and get their docket of jobs printed and out the door.

The warehouse became silent as the printing machines were turned to idle, a moment of calm that only occurred three times each day between shift changes. Fulton, carrying a clipboard with notes he had made from talking with the previous shift's supervisor, walked around each of the three large printing machines, visually inspecting them for any obvious problems. His shift's crew began filing into the warehouse, gathering in the center space created by the three large machines.

The work they did throughout the day wasn't particularly dangerous, but it was demanding. One member of each machine's team had to load up the specifications for the next order on the machine's software. In the meantime, the other two members loaded the printing material – paper, canvas, or any number of materials depending on the type and quantity of the orders. After the printing stock was loaded, they all had to monitor the output on the machine, noting whether the designs were being printed squarely, with the correct resolution, color balance, and dozens of other quality factors. When one order was done printing, the next run had to be loaded and ready to go, otherwise downtime on the machines would back up production into the next shift. A single change in any step of production would mean a different product and wasted materials. The company's leadership was thankful that Fulton was an expert in keeping things consistent on the production floor.

Fulton, on the other hand, was happy they had enough orders to keep the machine constantly running – it meant that the company's sales team was doing well. However, it did come with its own set of challenges, the least of which was regular maintenance. Running the machines almost nonstop five (and sometimes six) days a week meant each team had to be vigilant and catch potential problems before they happened. Malfunctions could waste valuable printing materials, inks, and most of all – time the machines could be turning out orders. It was an unexpected threat Fulton was committed to eliminating.

Over the months since he had taken over as shift supervisor, Fulton built upon the maintenance schedule he created. He also implemented checklists all the shifts could use so they had a standardized way of loading the orders, monitoring them for quality and transporting them to the rear docks of the warehouse so they could be loaded onto the delivery trucks and get out on time. The other two shift supervisors didn't use the checklists at first; they were, after all, senior to Fulton. However, when the operations manager noticed Fulton's increased output and decreased errors and wasted materials, he wanted to know how Fulton was doing it. Soon, all three shifts were using the checklists and the company's production jumped by 30%, while downtime for the machines was reduced by half. Orders were getting out the door on time. Customers were noticing the consistent quality of their printed materials and were beginning to refer the printing company to their peers and even their competitors. Changes still occurred, but now the shifts felt more prepared to deal with them.

While the printing company had definitely benefitted from Fulton's presence, there was one process that made Fulton's shift stand out above and beyond the other two. To an outsider, Fulton's crew just seemed to work better as a team. It wasn't that they anticipated the movements of each other or even the crews working the other two machines. However, they didn't need to stop during their shift to ask questions, get advice on how to fix problems, or stop production to transfer a job to another machine when one machine malfunctioned. It seemed that the teams just knew who was supposed to be where and what they were supposed to be doing. They counted on each other to be there at the right time for hand-offs, material loading, and shifting production to the correct machine when one went down. What appeared to be a sixth-sense among Fulton's shift was something Fulton had implemented the first day he reported for duty as a shift manager. It wasn't magic, and his crew wasn't telepathic. They were just more able to deal with unexpected change.

Fulton simply prepared his crew before each shift.

He finished making notes on his clipboard as the members of his shift gathered around him. They were used to this daily ritual before they began work. While some had initially balked at the idea of having 'another meeting' each day, they quickly found it gave them a structure that made their work more efficient and, surprisingly, easier. They waited patiently as their shift supervisor finished his notes and then looked at his wristwatch.

"It is 7:53, ladies and gentlemen. Hope everyone has had a great morning!" Fulton said. His crew smiled and nodded, returning the same pleasantries. "As we heard last week during our employee all-call, the company is on track to break over 10 million in revenue this year.

Expanding into large format printing has opened up some markets we weren't able to reach with our previous printing presses and has increased our margins considerably. Of course, the additional revenue means more work for us and by all accounts, we're doing well in handling it."

The shift was happy to hear this – if the company broke its ceiling of 10 million in revenue, their bonuses would double.

"Today, we have seventeen orders to print and three on backlog from the previous shift," Fulton told his crew. "Those three backed-up orders are due out today, so they are our priority. Our sales department is expecting the other seventeen to be ready to load for delivery at the end of our shift, and I don't expect we'll disappoint them."

The crew chuckled – like all companies with sales and production departments, the sales team was always promising the impossible to their clients. This left the fulfillment to the production team, which gave them the self-titled nickname 'miracle workers.'

"The third shift informed me that press number three went down an hour after their shift began, and it took them 45 minutes to get it back online," Fulton said, referencing his notes. "They repaired the problem but if you are working on press three, keep your eyes open to make sure the ink lines are running clearly. At the end of your shift, make sure to flush them as they're due for it anyway."

His crew assigned to press three nodded their acknowledgement.

"Additionally, we're going to be handling some billboard sectionals today. Our machines have a tendency to misalign those, so make sure you are inputting the correct numbers into the program before you load the materials," Fulton continued. "As you may know, April has just received her certification as to repair large format presses," Fulton shifted the clipboard under his arm and began clapping, which the team joined in on. "So I'm going to make sure she is on a team that doesn't have a certified technician in case their machine goes down. Our repair protocol will remain the same – the technician gets to work solving problems and the remaining members of the team work to shift printing material and design schematics to their assigned back-up printer."

The team nodded – each of them had experience with the potentially-hectic run-around that occurred when a machine went down. It had improved considerably since Fulton's checklists were adopted throughout the shifts, but it was still a potentially stressful experience. Many of his shift's members likened it to being in the pits during a car race. Everyone had a job, and if they worked together when a machine went down, it was like being part of a top-notch pit crew.

"As always, do your best to stick with your assigned position, either inputting schematics, loading material or working quality control," Fulton reminded the crew. "If you're getting bored, let me know after the shift, and I'll change your position for next week's schedule to keep it fresh for you."

"We're all familiar with what to do if a machine goes down, but I've also been told that we don't have all the materials needed for some canvas banners we need to complete today," Fulton informed the shift. "We're expecting the supplies in by ten o'clock on special order. We'll save those orders for the end. If the material isn't here by two this afternoon, then we won't let that change slow us down. We'll look and see what orders have come in so we can get them done and move those canvas banners to the next shift. My guess is they'll be here on time."

At this point, they expected Fulton to pause and ask the same question he asked at this point during all of their preparation sessions. He didn't disappoint them.

"Any clarifying questions?" Fulton asked his assembled crew.

"Did we get our inks restocked since yesterday?" asked one of the crew members. "We had a decent supply at the end of our shift, but I could see us scraping the barrel by the end of our shift today."

"Great question. Once everyone gets started, I'll check our supply levels. And if we need to be restocked, I'll get more ink brought over from our storage room," Fulton said. "Anything else?"

When he didn't see anyone else with a question, Fulton turned and looked at his watch again.

"Alright team, you have five minutes to review your production checklists. When you're good to go, fire up your press and let's get to work," Fulton said.

Less than five minutes later, the silence in the warehouse ended as the machines sprang to life, echoing with a low roar as they warmed. Fulton liked the sound of the three machines going at once. It reminded him of the sound of tires on pavement – a sound he had come to love in the military. He walked from machine to machine checking ink levels and making more notes. His crew was busy loading the raw materials into the presses and inputting the schematics produced by their design department had and approved by their clients. As the first series of pictures began to appear from the output feeds of the large printers, Fulton turned away from the members of his shift and began walking toward the supply room to grab more ink containers. Fulton remembered that he'd seen some boxes of donuts and coffee in the break room on the way in.

"I'll make sure to bring everyone something when I come back in, even if it takes me away from the production floor a little longer," Fulton told himself.

He knew that any last-minute changes that came up in his absence would be handled. His shift was prepared.

PERFORM

Photo By Author, Dead Man's Patrol Entry into Fallujah, Iraq 2004

THE MISSION: PERFORM, PART I

June 13, 2004
Fallujah, Iraq

Corporal Lowis sat in the rear passenger seat of the Humvee as it rolled over the potholes that peppered the main supply route into Fallujah. He knew that each of the potholes had been made by the impact of weapons – mortars, improvised explosive devices, rockets and hand grenades – since the Marines and Army had begun patrolling the city the year prior. The patrol of 15 vehicles he was in had left the safety of the barbed-wire gate of the Camp Fallujah compound more than 20 minutes ago. As the vehicles rolled along the four-lane road that served as a highway in Iraq, Lowis noticed the city around him was deserted. Not a person in sight. The vehicles that were parked or disabled along the sides of the highway were abandoned. None of this boded well for his patrol. Whenever Lowis had gone into a town and not seen the typically bustling markets, or men lounging in the shade to avoid working in the sun, trouble quickly followed. Knowing this, Lowis tightened his grip on his M-16A2 rifle, which rested on the windowsill of the Humvee. He thought of how far he had come in just three years, a journey that had led him to this mission – the Dead Man's Patrol.

Lowis showed an aptitude for systems and understanding complex patterns – a rarity for someone without a college education. The Marines chose him for their language studies program. So while his basic training platoon-mates had gone off to infantry school or other occupational-specific training, Lowis had been sent to Monterey, California to the military's 64-week Arabic training course. While Monterey was a nice place to learn a foreign language, the Marine Corps had other locations in mind for Lowis. Upon graduating, he was sent to work for the intelligence unit of the 2nd Marine Expeditionary Force, located at Camp Lejeune, NC. When the Marines there were mobilized to support Operation Iraqi Freedom in the winter of 2002, Lowis was attached to an infantry battalion and sent into the field. He spent his first deployment translating between generals and tribal leaders in Iraq, a job he enjoyed. He quickly discovered the Arabic he was taught in school wasn't always spoken by Arabic people – much like the United States, there were many geographically-unique dialects. And like the English spoken in the United States, sometimes the dialects were difficult – if not impossible – to understand. The Arabic culture Lowis was responsible for being familiar with was much different from the culture he grew up in. For example, meetings often had to take place between people a half-dozen times before they ever got around to broaching the purpose of the meeting, something that infuriated the impatient Americans. Lowis understood if these two diametrically-opposed cultures were going to communicate, he would have to do more than translate what was being said word-for-word. He became adept at understanding the nuances of the language and dialects. He could also advise the officers about what should come next in a negotiation from a cultural perspective in addition to translating what was being said – and what wasn't being said. The top leaders learned that when Lowis was in the room translating, things tended to go smoother and more got done. For his second deployment, he was attached directly to General Mathis' staff.

It was that turn of events that landed him on what he found out was called the 'Dead Man's Patrol.' His job would be to accompany General Mathis into the negotiation room where he and another translator –

who happened to also be an intelligence officer – would monitor the negotiations. Lowis was their ace-in-the-hole. He would not be translating directly but would instead act as a security guard for the general until he heard that a settlement had been reached. At that point, he would leave the meeting room and brief the platoon commander outside so he could radio headquarters with the news. It was a simple plan, but it had a lot of unknown possibilities for the 21 year-old translator.

First, there was the slim chance the patrol would even arrive at the city center. Every coalition patrol that had entered the city in the last five months had been engaged, and none had made it as far as they were planning on going. Second, no one knew what to expect when they did enter the meeting room. Would be general be taken hostage? Would the tribal leaders be armed or have security of their own? Third, would the patrol make it out of the city in one piece? Lowis was aware the general was the top priority, and if things got messy, he would be extracted and Lowis would remain behind with the infantrymen in the patrol. Although he knew they were well-trained, the thought of the few dozen of them fighting their way out of a city of 300,000 angry people didn't fill him with confidence.

As the patrol passed the outskirts and began to enter into the main part of the city, Lowis looked out of the window and saw multiple Howitzer artillery guns, all pointed up at a high angle. Lowis knew that meant their rounds would be aimed less than a few miles away – what forward observers called 'danger close.' Their own patrol would be in danger of being hit if the rounds were fired. Although Lowis couldn't see them, he could hear FA-18s above. They would be providing overwatch, monitoring the live feed from the fixed-wing drones that floated above the tallest buildings of the city. As the patrol moved down the main supply route that flowed like an artery into the city center, Lowis saw three Huey helicopters pass above them, scouting their route and checking the rooftops. Snipers and rocket-propelled grenades were a huge danger in urban patrols and the Marines didn't always have air support. At that moment, Lowis was glad they were carrying a general and had a view of the rooftops and road ahead. The pilots were sending regular updates through their radios to the vehicle commander in the patrol.

The driver of Lowis' vehicle had his eyes on the vehicle ahead of him, constantly checking spacing and speed. The Humvees were dispersed such that if an improvised explosive device was triggered, the damage to the surrounding vehicles wouldn't be lethal. Lowis and the other Marines had learned in 2003 that bunching the vehicles up made for an easier target for their enemies to attack. Although they couldn't stop someone from placing an IED, they could ensure the damage to their patrol was minimal.

Beside the driver sat the platoon sergeant, a wiry man with intelligent eyes who also had his rifle resting on the windowsill of the Humvee. He was talking to the other Humvee drivers on his headset radio, checking in occasionally with the forward-air controller who was, in turn, in contact with the Hueys and FA-18s above them. Each of them had been briefed – their primary mission objective was to get the general into the city center, provide as much security as they were able, and get him out safely. In addition to that, they had to worry about protecting each other, covering interlocking fields of fire from their vehicles, and performing their individual duties, whether it was leadership – as in the platoon sergeant's case – or as a translator – like Fulton. On top of that was the fact they were behind enemy lines in hostile territory. The moving pieces, overwhelming risks and dozens of possible changes to their plan were enough to drive anyone crazy.

"We've got reports of small arms fire on the south side of the city, but it might be celebratory so we're pressing on," the platoon sergeant told the patrol through his radio.

Celebratory fire – firing small arms like pistols and AK-47s into the air – was akin to fireworks back in America. The Marines were used to Iraqis celebrating by popping off a few rounds. The only difference between them and the fireworks back home was small arms fire could also be used to coordinate an impending attack. Each Marine was on guard, their thumbs resting on the safety switches of their rifles, or, in the case of the mounted gunner that stood in the back of the Humvees, an empty shell casing that prevented the trigger plate from being depressed. The Marines knew that if they accidentally opened fire in the middle of the city, it could be the same as signing their death warrant.

Lowis breathed deeply, remembering his training. With all that was going on, he could only completely focus on one thing at a time. At that moment, it wasn't what would happen when they arrived – his translator duties – or how they were going to fight their way back out of the city if need be. Right now, it was covering his sector of fire from the Humvee. His eyes scanned the windows, doorways and alleys of the buildings outside his windows, on guard for any threats.

"Ten mikes to arrival," the platoon sergeant said into his radio to the patrol vehicles, using the military's jargon for 'ten minutes.' Lowis kept his eyes on the alleys and rooftops. He still hadn't seen a single soul – it was like all 300,000 residents of the desert city had evaporated in the morning's heat.

In what seemed like just a few seconds from when they entered the city, the patrol rolled to a stop outside a large building that could have passed for a courthouse or government office in a medium-sized American town. A large parking lot in the front of the building ended with a series of concrete steps that led to a series of double doors. The Humvees formed a semicircle around the steps leading to the building. The machine gunners spun their weapons to face out, while the Marines dismounted and covered a sector of fire facing toward the street and buildings ahead. Lowis and the other Marines saw where the majority of the residents of Fallujah had been. It seemed like all 300,000 of them – mostly military-aged males from the look of it – were gathering in the buildings across from and to the sides of the city center. They were seated in the windowsills, on the front steps and on rooftops. They were standing everywhere they could fit a person on the sidewalks and in the alleys. In any other situation, the Marines would have felt like celebrities. However, from the looks in the Iraqis' eyes and the dead silence that hung over the crowd, the Marines felt anything but welcome.

Lowis exited his Humvee and jogged to meet General Mathis and the other translator as they bounded up the front steps of the building. The Marines were all aware the longer they stood outside, the more of a target they would be for any trigger-happy insurgents in the surrounding buildings. As they entered the shade and darkness of the city center's interior, they were met by a line of Arabs all wearing the keffiyeh, or patterned headdress of a Muslim who has made the hajj, the pilgrimage to Mecca. That immediately told Lowis that he was dealing with men of means. The journey was not a cheap one from Iraq – these men had some resources, and therefore, power. Their presence at this negotiation confirmed it.

The three Marines, still wearing their helmets and body armor, stepped into a large conference room. Flat pillows were lined up against the walls with a raised bench large enough for three men to sit comfortably at the head of the table. It was this bench the sheikhs led the general to. He unbuckled his helmet and removed it as he greeted the tribal leaders filing into the room after him. The second translator, the intelligence officer, made introductions and translated the greetings from the tribal leaders. The head of the city's militia – and de facto spokesman – offered just enough of a greeting to not be rude and then sat on the bench, leaving just adequate space for the general and his translator.

Things were going well thus far. The group assumed the officer was the general's aide and hardly gave Lowis a second glance.

Lowis staged himself to the left of the room's double door, listening intently for any side conversations that might be useful for their intelligence officers when he returned. He wasn't focused on security outside the room – he left that to the Marines stationed outside. There weren't enough of them to hold off the crowd if it decided to attack, but the Iraqis had kept their end of the bargain to hold the cease-fire. Now, his job was to gather all the information he could about the people in the room and what they said – both within and outside of the general's earshot.

While there was an undercurrent of tension in the room, things started out amicably enough. Pleasantries were exchanged and then the leaders got down to business — what could they do to get their power and water turned back on? General Mathis tried his best to explain that he needed to be able to freely move coalition troops throughout the city, but the tribal leaders stood their ground. Why should they, the leaders asked, who had the largest militia in Iraq, need Marines and soldiers patrolling their streets? They could keep their people safe and enforce order, they insisted.

Lowis was used to this line of reasoning — he had heard it from countless tribal leaders for more than a year. Even though many Iraqis were living in squalor, they were very proud and wanted to ensure the coalition forces knew they could keep order in their cities. The general and his interpreter conceded the leaders could keep their people safe, and then offered to bring in medicine and other supplies that would raise the community's quality of life. Patrols would be limited to just those needed to protect the supply convoys. This was something the tribal leaders were interested in — enough to agree to a 3-week ceasefire so the supplies could be delivered, and their electricity and water turned back on.

When an agreement was struck, Lowis had the cue he was waiting for. He turned to the back wall, and as silently as he could, opened one of the double doors and slipped out into the dark hallway that led to the front of the building. When he stepped into the sunlight, the platoon sergeant was waiting for him. His back was pointed towards the darkness, and he was staring through his sunglasses to the buildings across the street.

"What do you have for me?" the man asked. After Lowis explained what he had heard, the platoon sergeant jogged to his Humvee, quickly speaking into his radio to relay the message back to headquarters. Lowis cut across the semicircle made by the parked Humvees and walked back to the Humvee he had arrived in, asking one of the other Marines what the situation was out here.

"It's hairy as hell, almost enough to scare somebody," the Marine responded. Lowis thought this was a slightly odd statement coming from a young man who was standing behind a machine gun with a barrel just less than 4 feet long that fired bullets so large they literally separated their targets, but he understood his fellow Marine's sentiments. The men who were crowding the buildings across from them had begun moving into the alleys and in front of the buildings. A few AK-47s could be seen hung from shoulder straps and concealed behind robes. If a firefight broke out here, things could get very ugly, very quickly. Not just for the Marines, but for the general and his translator. It was a threat they had considered, but not one that ended well for the Marines.

"Where do you need another rifle?" Lowis asked the Marine standing above him in the Humvee.

"Cover our left flank. We need someone over there," the Marine replied, nodding his head towards the left side of the semicircle.

Lowis walked behind the Humvees, past the mounted Marines and those who had their rifles resting on the hoods and tailgates of their vehicles. He took his place on the tailgate of the last vehicle on the left, and stared out at the men in the building across from him, each meeting his gaze with what Lowis thought was an angry, silent intent. The patrol had made it farther than any coalition patrol had in quite a while – the Iraqis saw it as an incursion into their neighborhoods.

A few seconds later, someone grabbed the back of Lowis' flak jacket and spun him around. It was the platoon sergeant, and by the scowl on his face, he looked none too happy.

"What are you doing out here?!" the platoon sergeant demanded in a coarse whisper. Even though it wasn't loud, Lowis could hear the anger behind it.

"Keeping watch over the left sector and waiting for the general to exit, staff sergeant." Lowis replied.

"I guess you didn't get the word, but you're needed back in there," the platoon sergeant said, gesturing toward the entrance of the building. He continued, "The only Marine in there to cover the general is armed with just a pistol. I want you back in there."

"The plan was to have the translator provide security," Lowis said. "What are my new orders?"

The platoon sergeant leaned down until he was inches away from Lowis' face.

"If anyone goes for the general, you do whatever you have to do to keep him safe," the platoon sergeant whispered is a rasp.

Lowis understood. This was a massive change in the plan for the young translator, but he didn't miss a step as he headed back into the building. The mounted guns and rifles of the Marines outside each shifted a little to the left to make up for the space Lowis had been covering a moment before. They had spent countless hours in training doing that very thing – shifting their fields of fire to cover any gaps that might open, either from a Marine being called away or from being taken out of action.

Lowis headed back down the shadowy hall and slowly opened the door to the large meeting room. Some heads turned as they heard the door open. But because Lowis had been in the room minutes before, everyone turned back to the general, his translator and the head sheikh as they wrapped up negotiations. Lowis stood against the back wall, his hand on the handle of his rifle, his finger off the trigger so as not to cause concern or appear to aggressive to the men in the room.

When the meeting was concluded, the three Marines headed back to their vehicles, the general in the lead, flanked by his translator and Lowis. Within seconds, the patrol was pulling their vehicles back onto the main supply route and headed back to Camp Fallujah. As the vehicles left the city center behind, they could see the flood of people waiting in the surrounding buildings move into the street. They formed a wall in the road and in front of the city center. There was no way the Marines were going to get back in there when the streets looked like a stadium emptying after a big game. Each of the Marines in the patrol were relieved they hadn't been called up to bat in that game.

The Humvees retained their distancing all the way back to the camp. As soon as the patrol passed the artillery cannons, Lowis saw the battery's

Marines begin packing up their gear to get it far outside the range of any snipers hiding in the buildings ahead of them. The infantry troops did the same, rallying into their troop transport vehicles and Humvees to get back to the safety of Camp Fallujah.

On the wall of Camp Fallujah, the guards were ready to receive the patrol and the barbed-wire fence gate rolled open, flanked on either side by six-foot high walls of sandbags. The concrete-and-barbed-wire-compound wasn't much, but for these Marines it was home.

The small patrol drove back to the south end of the camp, leaving the blacktop to roll back into the staging positions they began in that morning. As they circled up where they had disembarked earlier, Lewis shook his head in disbelief. They had just travelled to the middle of the hornet's nest, riled it up with a great big stick, and made it out without a scratch. It was the first time anyone could remember such a thing happening with a patrol in Fallujah-

Not. One. Shot. Fired.

THE BUSINESS: PERFORM, PART II

March 1, 2014
Tampa, FL

Tyler Lowis cranked the air conditioning in his car to full blast as he and his sales team prepared to leave the lot of their office. After sitting in the sun all morning, the leather seats were hot to the touch. They slowly began to cool as the car gained speed and merged onto the interstate, the air conditioning eventually making progress against Florida's summer heat. The team was headed out to make what was perhaps one of their most important presentations ever to a client that they'd been working to get in front of for months. It was do-or-die, and Lowis hoped his folks were ready.

After his enlistment in the Marines, Lowis used the G.I. Bill to get a bachelor's degree in history, minoring in Arabic studies. While his original plan was to go on to pursue a doctoral degree and teach at a university, the extra years of needed education were too much of a wait for him. After his tours in Iraq, he was eager to get started with the rest of his life. He took his degree and tried his hand at what he was told had the highest potential for increased income – business-to-business sales.

Contrary to what he thought when he applied for the job, his history degree was not a waste of time— the research skills he had learned were helpful in studying his prospects' companies. The first sales job he took was ideally suited to his experiences – a company selling IT consulting to organizations in a largely Arabic-speaking business district. While not responsible for delivering the IT consulting services himself, he was responsible for business development and closing increasingly larger deals. Instead of working as a lone wolf, he was placed on a team that included an analyst, a software developer and an IT systems trainer. Each of his team members were responsible for executing part of the sales presentation, as well as answering questions about their services to their prospects. Except for Lowis, they were also partially responsible for delivering services to the client. Although Lowis rarely had to use the Arabic language when communicating during presentations, the cultural lessons he'd learned in Iraq served him well with his prospects. With his team behind him, Lowis figured that making the type of complex sales his company sought would be easy.

He was wrong.

First, the company had no sales standards to speak of – no guidance for how presentations should be made or how to tailor them to individual prospects. This meant that each team was left to create their own way of doing business on the fly. Some of the teams, through luck or chance, were achieving consistently better numbers than their peers each month. When asked what they were doing differently, these high-performing teams could only point to the experience of their individual members. This infuriated the leaders at the consulting firm, because they couldn't replicate individual experience. As a result, the IT firm's leaders brought in sales trainers, motivational speakers, and customer-relationship management systems, all in a vain attempt to replicate the success of their top-performers.

Second, Lowis found the sales teams across the organization were plagued by the same challenges. From getting lost on the way, showing up late to their meetings, to audio-visual equipment issues immediately destroying their credibility, they would usually create more obstacles to their success than their prospects ever could with objections. Although each of these challenges seemed new to the team experiencing them, they actually occurred across the sales department. If there was anything Lowis noticed about the high performers that was different than other teams, it was the high performers knew how to deal with these common challenges.

Third, their firm was in a competitive industry and their prospects were bombarded with consulting companies' marketing efforts. Everyone was constantly trying to get an increasingly thinner piece of the pie. This made it difficult to not compete on price. Once a proposal was delivered, it was not uncommon for their prospects to replicate the proposed work and bid out to their competitors. Selling a commodity with a five or six-figure price tag was not a business Lowis wanted to be in, but was a challenge he was determined to overcome.

Eight days prior to getting in the car with his team, Lowis had neither time nor luck on his side. If this next presentation was going to be successful, he knew it was up to him to make it that way. As the lead on this account, he had done everything he knew to do in gathering information on the prospect – their financials, their goals, even the product launches they had in their pipeline. It was the same research he had done on all the other accounts that didn't buy. He knew he had a good team behind him, a team that knew their stuff. So what changes would he make in the stressful moments leading up to the presentation and while in front of the prospects? Whatever challenges that came up, he needed his team to be confident they were ready for them.

As he sat pondering this in his office, Lowis wondered where else he had seen complex operations that rapidly adapted to challenges. It didn't take long for him to remember that he had spent years doing that very thing when he was attached with Marine Corps units in the field. Just like sales, those missions had involved complex environments with multiple players and challenging environments. Additionally, he had worked with specialists who had to know when their skills were needed without being told. He picked up a notebook and began writing out a version of an action plan like those he had seen in the military.

When Lowis met with his team the next day to go over his notes, he knew this time around they'd do something different than 'show up and throw up.' Instead of winging it like he and the other teams were used to doing, he decided to create a plan that accounted for the challenges they'd likely face. First, Lowis decided he didn't need a sale, he just needed an advance. This meant the team would be successful if they achieved anything from a sale to a meeting with the entire decision-making team. The key to success would be in how his team executed – and Lowis knew that this time it wouldn't be in a haphazard way. He'd tried that and needed to change the way his team approached every aspect of the presentation. He needed more reliable results.

Lowis looked at each member of his team and laid out his plan.

"We all understand we're looking for an advance with this prospect. So we're going to change the way we approach this. We need to do everything possible to understand what their IT needs are and make sure we present ourselves not as a sales team but as expert advisors," Lowis told the assembled group. "And the first thing they'll look for when we step into the room is competence. That impression starts long before the meeting itself, and involves preparing in advance so last-minute problems don't trip us up."

Lowis explained to his team that the worst thing that could happen was they spend half an hour scouring the building, trying to find the right floor, the right department and the right meeting room.

"Tom, because you'll be the one responsible for training their office staff in how to use the new systems if we close the deal, I want you to recon and locate the meeting room in the next few days. We have the location confirmed – I want to make sure you know exactly where we'll need to park and how to get to that meeting room," Lowis told his systems trainer. He continued, "Make sure you time your trip so we know how much time to allow from our office to their parking garage, and from there to the meeting room. While you're in the building, drop in on our prospect's administrative assistant. Explain you'd like to gather some information from their IT department to make sure you make the most of their leaders' time. Get what you need to find out what they're currently using, what they've tried recently, how well it worked and what they wish could be better. Make sure you share that with us prior to the day of the appointment."

Tom nodded, taking notes. He'd normally found all of this information out from the prospect during the meeting. Sometimes it was a tough slog, as decision makers weren't always familiar with the systems they were currently using. Getting this information ahead of time would be a big help in speaking to the customer's needs.

Lowis then turned to his analyst.

"Barry, I need you to reach out to the other analysts and get some copies of the slide decks they used in their successful sales. The decks should be on our network drives, which will make them easy to find. Combine them into a flow that makes sense for presenting to this particular prospect. I'll send you my research on the company later today."

Barry had been using a slide deck he built in the past for his first prospect. It would be interesting to see not only what information his peers had generated for their prospects, but also how they had set up the stories of what they could deliver in the slides.

Lowis then turned to his software developer.

"Jenn, you'll be there to answer questions about how the prospect's existing software will integrate with any new platforms we create for them. And I know you're busy working on other accounts, so the biggest thing I need you to make sure our audiovisual equipment is set and ready to go for the day of the presentation." He added, "Test everything the day prior on our gear – and make sure we're bringing our own laptop and projector just in case the one in the room we're in goes down."

Heads around the table nodded – each of them had specific tasks to accomplish before the meeting in a week. Although it was work they weren't used to doing, they all shared in a portion of the commission.

Each of them had a stake in the game.

When his team dispersed, Lowis knew he had handled the first part of their performance – setting themselves up so they would appear to be credible and professional. The real challenge would be to deliver on that impression by serving as advisors and subject-matter experts.

With this objective in mind, Lowis asked himself – Who will handle what parts of the presentation? What happens when a question comes up? Who will handle answering it? Lowis had been in many presentations where team members had interrupted each other, sometimes even contradicting one another. Almost unbelievably, Lowis had also seen teams openly argue with one another about the faults of one platform they were proposing in front of their prospect. He was determined that his team wouldn't make those mistakes.

Many of the questions Lowis anticipated from his prospects were technical in nature. While he could take a stab at an answer, he wanted these prospects to perceive their team as subject-matter experts. Lowis figured it should be the software developer who handled questions of a technical nature. For questions regarding implementing their solutions across the prospect's teams of employees – that was the trainer's realm. Lowis was a trained educator, but he knew that wasn't the same as being able to project out implementation dates and spin-up timeframes. While Lowis understood enough about business to speak to leaders, he couldn't project financial forecasts based on return-on-investment for software applications, so he would leave any financial questions to the analyst on the team. The trick was planning the presentation well enough so each of his team members knew when to speak and who would address which questions. He wanted the person with experience in their area to answer. Lowis spent the evening mapping out every question he could remember hearing from prospects since his first sales call with the company. He then separated them out by role and forwarded them onto his individual teammates.

The next morning, Barry had reviewed the slide decks from the other teams and formed his own. Lowis sat down with the analyst to chart out not how their IT consulting could make their prospect's company more profitable, but rather how the prospect should go about choosing an IT consulting firm to deliver service in the first place. It was an odd strategy to Barry, but Lowis was confident in it.

"The one thing our top teams are doing," Lowis told Barry, "is bringing a whole lot of experience in delivering these solutions to their prospects. I've listened to their recorded presentations, when they do record them, and you know what I found out?"

Barry shook his head back and forth in response.

"I found they spent more time talking about developing a buying and implementation strategy for general IT projects the company was considering, rather than focusing on the features and benefits of our IT solutions."

Lowis knew if they were going to be perceived as subject-matter experts, they would have to build their presentation to position themselves as advisors to their clients and not just as a group looking to make a sale.

Another major challenge teams in his company faced was one person trying to carry all the duties of the team during the whole presentation. Often one person was running the slide deck, talking with clients, mapping decision trees on a whiteboard and handing out any material they asked for. Therefore, prospects spent most of the meeting time waiting, and the team appeared unprofessional as they shuffled materials around, trying to find the document the prospect asked for. It was a simple challenge to overcome, if his team prepared for it in advance.

This presentation was going to be different. Lowis assigned each member of his team a primary role around their business function. Then he assigned a secondary role around what they would be doing when they weren't actively engaged in a discussion with the prospect – running the slide deck, pulling data from their three-ring resource notebook, scribing on the whiteboard – all the things that typically fell on one person or were clumsily shuffled around. Lowis knew if his team was able to remember their primary and secondary duty during the presentation, they would be able operate as a single entity, just as his units had on the battlefield. They would come across as a single entity totally dedicated to providing their prospects value – exactly how Lowis wanted his team to be perceived.

It was a lot for one person to remember, so Lowis had the team get together the day prior to the actual prospect meeting for a dry run. In Iraq, he'd sat in a Humvee with no air conditioning for hours while the drivers practiced evasive maneuvers and proper spacing. This dry run was in an air-conditioned office in the IT consulting firm's board room.

The team loaded their slide deck onto the laptop in the large room and realized the platform it was built on wasn't compatible with the laptop's operating system. Lowis made a note to himself and Barry to load versions of the deck that were compatible with all major operating systems they were likely to encounter.

Next, an employee from another sales team took the place of the prospect and Lowis practiced his opening statement, getting feedback from the team member. As he began to speak, Jenn clicked through the slides at the appropriate time.

The 'prospect' asked a question about how the IT consulting firm's work would integrate with their existing software, and Jenn moved away from the computer to answer. While she was talking with their 'prospect,' Lowis clicked through the deck until he came to the page with the data and figures that Jenn was referencing. When Jenn had answered their 'prospect's' question, she returned to running the slide deck while Lowis took over.

Aside from a few hiccups which Lowis noted, their dry-run presentation went well. They identified a half-dozen challenges and corrected them in the comfort of their office and not in a high-stress environment in front of their prospect. Tom had located the meeting room in the company they would be visiting tomorrow. He had also written instructions on how to get there in case he was pulled away from the appointment for some reason. Lowis' team was as prepared as they would ever be. All that was left to do was execute his plan.

As their car pulled into the prospect's parking garage, they were waved through by a security guard. Tom, as he had warned, was pulled away on another project at the last minute. Without his written guidance, they would have been late and lost. Tom had instructed them to go to the fourth level of the parking deck as that was where a sky bridge would give them easiest access to the client building. Lowis parked the car on that level and the team members grabbed their equipment and made their way across the covered bridge.

Tom's instructions deftly guided them around turns in hallways, making their way through the labyrinth of cubicles with ease. They found their prospect's office and checked in with the administrative assistant who showed them to the meeting room. It was empty except for a long meeting table, high-backed chairs and a pitcher of water with glasses. No laptop to plug their presentation into.

"Whew, glad we brought our own laptop as a backup!" Lowis thought. Lowis and Jenn began setting up the audio-visual equipment, plugging their own laptop into the projector's cables.

They had ten minutes to prepare the room, unlike so many of their previous presentations where every minute prior was spent in a mad dash, rushing from one wing or tower of a complex in an attempt to find the right room. No one from their team was hurrying in at the last minute, sweaty and nervous.

Lowis and his team arranged the chairs so his two prospects would sit in the place of honor facing the screen, not staring into the bright light outside the windows. They also adjusted the lights so everyone could see the projector's screen and each other – neither too bright nor too dark. The worst presentations Lowis had been part of were conducted in shadowy rooms. With everything set, the team reviewed their primary and secondary roles one last time. The door to the meeting room opened and their prospects walked in – it was go time.

As the team left the office, they knew this presentation had gone much differently than the ones they had been part of in the past. For one thing, the prospects had never asked them about their billing rate – in fact, price hadn't come up once. Lowis' team had started by going over the current systems and platforms the prospect company used – information Tom had gathered during his visit the week prior. The executives complained about the problems they were encountering with it, and Jenn was quick to respond and explain why the platforms weren't integrating as well together as they should. This led into a conversation about finding a solution to tie all their disparate systems together, a different (and potentially more profitable) solution than the team had originally planned to discuss.

Barry was perfectly suited to answer those questions. The slide deck he built spoke more to making the prospect's company more profitable with a shared platform than about the IT consulting firm's history, accolades or high-profile clients.

Next, the two executives wanted to know about what the timeline for creating a shared platform would be – normally an opportunity Lowis would have jumped on as an invitation to sell his firm's consulting programs. Barry and Jenn were about to jump in when Lowis put his hand on Barry shoulder to silence him, never breaking eye contact with the prospects. The plan was about to change.

"That's a great question, sir," Lowis said. "I'd like to answer it by telling you exactly how long not only my firm would take, but the timelines and capabilities you'll get from the other IT consulting firms in town. Would that be helpful?"

The executives nodded their heads in agreement. Anything to save them the time of meeting with multiple firms was a blessing.

Lowis then told the executives not what platform would be best for them or how long it would take to implement, but rather how to choose the right platform for the company's long-term growth goals. This impressed the executives, and the team had the materials to educate the two of them on the timeline and expectations ready to go. Barry took over the slide deck while Jenn pulled the notebooks from her briefcase and handed them to their prospects. Lowis walked the executives through the notebooks, outlining the pros and cons of each solution that would tie their individual platforms together. He also explained how their IT consulting firm, and the others in town, would assess and deliver each of them.

The executives invited the team to share their thoughts with the organization's CEO at next week's board meeting.

As Lowis' team pulled out of the parking lot, he smiled. As stressful as the presentation could have been, his team had performed like they were having a friendly chat with largest client in their consulting company's history.

If the meeting with the CEO went well next week, they would be.

PROCESS

Photo By Lance Cpl. Scott Whiting, USMC

THE MISSION: PROCESS, PART I

June 13, 2004
South Compound, Camp Fallujah, Iraq

C aptain MacRae let out a huge sigh of relief when he saw the Humvees drive into the company motor pool, and, in a cloud of dust, cut the power to their engines. It had been a long day for all the Marines at Camp Fallujah. The field surgeons had their triage and surgery centers prepared, expecting massive casualties. All the intelligence units were busy monitoring their drone feeds and ground intelligence assets for any word about the patrol. Every infantry unit was on alert, waiting for the order to jump into their vehicles and head toward to city to extract the patrol from one of the safe houses. MacRae himself had been sitting with the headset of his radio pressed against his ear for the last four hours, listening to all the radio traffic from the patrol that no one was expected to return from. It was late afternoon, and the Marines returning from the patrol were eager to begin unloading the ammunition, water and food they had brought with them in expectation for a long fight inside Fallujah. But according to all reports, not a single shot had been fired.

Hardly anyone at Camp Fallujah, the forward-operating base the Marines lived and worked out of, could believe what had just happened – or hadn't happened – on the patrol. For the last several months they had seen patrol after patrol limp back into the compound – sometimes with less vehicles than they left with. The fact that everyone made it back safely was reason enough to celebrate – the fact that General Mathis was still among them was enough to cause a person to jump for joy. Marines, of course, were more reserved than that. However, there wasn't one among them at the forward operating base who wasn't happy about staying in the relative comfort of their tents that day.

MacRae watched as the Marines from the patrol jumped off their vehicles and began guzzling the cool water waiting for them at their company staging area. Even though the sun had passed its zenith, the temperature was still close to 107 degrees Fahrenheit. At that temperature, sweat immediately evaporated from the skin and left their uniforms bone dry. When combined with traveling in a moving vehicle pounded by desert wind, dehydration became as constant of a threat to the Marines as the insurgents they were fighting. When one factored in the adrenaline that came as part of the job, it was easy to see how they could go through hundreds of gallons of fresh water a day.

General Mathis exited his Humvee and went from vehicle to vehicle, thanking the Marines for doing a good job, for completing the mission. At their forward operating base, saluting was not allowed due to the threat of snipers. Officers were always high-value targets and saluting immediately identified them to any watchful marksman outside the compound. This was a lesson the Marines had learned during the Revolutionary War, and was trained into them so no officer would be unnecessarily targeted. However, the Marines still popped to attention whenever the general approached. After he made his way to the last vehicle, he passed by MacRae, who also came to attention as the general passed. General Mathis stepped into the company tent to grab water and a radio, filing a situation report to his boss – the theater commander, a four-star Army general in Baghdad. The Marines at the vehicles didn't disperse for showers and food, however. They knew their mission wasn't done yet. They still had to deal with MacRae.

MacRae liked to think of himself as the 'innovation officer,' but he knew that title wasn't entirely accurate, because he didn't really innovate anything. His job was, however, to record the innovative things Marines did. MacRae was present at the end of every one of their missions, every patrol and every operation to conduct an after-action session with the Marines. There, he would find out what had gone right, what had gone wrong and what they could do better next time. In a training environment, his job was sometimes monotonous as they went over the same lessons the previous platoon had learned – but in combat things were different. On the best days, he was surprised that the Marines he debriefed had been so brilliant under pressure. For instance, they had once created mobile bridges to travel from rooftop to rooftop using only a small ladder that served as a catwalk. On the worst days, the after-action reports stretched out, adrenaline garbling the Marines' speech as MacRae asked them to process the attacks they had just survived.

It was vital these lessons were compiled as soon as the Marines returned – even a few hours would blur their memories, and MacRae needed them to remember every detail of their missions. Each detail may be the difference between success and failure for the next unit attempting a similar mission. Even though MacRae rarely went on patrol himself, he realized the importance of his role. He was the continuity that linked the Marines at his forward operating base to Marines and coalition forces all over the Middle East. Each of the after-action sessions he facilitated were immediately shared across the globe.

Today's session would be a good one, MacRae knew. Not only was a high-value target involved – General Mathis – but the patrol also went in without heavy armor for support. In an ideal world, every patrol would be able to handle themselves as well as this one did – get in, complete their mission, and get out without engaging the enemy or needing tanks, rockets, working dogs, or any of the other resources patrols often requested. Most importantly, the patrol hadn't suffered any casualties. While it was not uncommon for these patrols to come back unscathed, there was always an exchange of fire. If there were a few things this team did to ensure no one shot at them, it would be valuable for all the other coalition forces in Iraq and Afghanistan to know.

The Marine Corps had a long history of gathering this type of information – it had become extremely useful in staying a step ahead of their competition. Because each patrol would take the time to share their lessons learned, their enemies could only use a tactic on them once. After that, the Marines who fought their way out of it, or a separate committee, would develop a way to counter the tactic and share that information across the entire theater of operations. When computers became available to store and share information, the Marine Corps was one of the first branches to take advantage of their database capability. They had developed a platform called MCLLS – the Marine Corps Lesson Learned System. MacRae, along with other officers and non-commissioned officers like him, were responsible for gathering, sorting through, and inputting the raw data needed to make MCLLS a much-respected tool for all Marines in their planning and briefing sessions. It was respected because the resource saved lives.

MacRae greeted the Marines as they approached him. He was joined outside the canvas tent that served as the company headquarters by representatives from the artillery battery and air support unit that were directing the efforts of the Howitzers, Hueys, unmanned drones and FA-18s overhead. Their input would help create a fuller picture of how the mission was accomplished.

As the group of Marines circled up around MacRae, he could detect a faint smile on each one of their faces – as if they had all just cheated death. MacRae understood why they would feel that way. As was typical, they reserved their celebrating for later when they were off duty. Now it was time for business. Each of the Marines were familiar with the after-action process and waited for MacRae to begin.

"All right, gents, first – welcome back. Outstanding job!" MacRae told the assembled warriors.

"Ooorah!" they responded in unison. (Note: The actual response Marines make is somewhere between a dog's bark and a guttural shout. No written word has been discovered that accurately describes it.)

"Let's get rolling. Staff sergeant, give me an overview of the mission as you executed it," MacRae said to the platoon sergeant standing in the middle of the men.

"Roger that, sir," Staff Sgt. Fulton said as he stepped forward. "We were tasked with safely transporting General Mathis to the town center where he would conduct negotiations with the natives, and then we were tasked with getting him back safely."

"Sounds good," MacRae said.

MacRae was holding a clipboard with the basic information he had received about the patrol from their headquarters staff. He listened carefully to Fulton's response, ensuring it matched with what he had been told. One of the easiest mistakes when conducting an after-action report was to have a misunderstanding of the primary objective. It was rare, but sometimes a confusing or misunderstood objective meant the Marines executed the wrong mission. Thankfully, the team had a good staff non-commissioned officer overseeing things. What he said matched perfectly with what MacRae had on his clipboard.

"Next, tell me the flow of the mission, the courses of action you followed," MacRae instructed.

"We left on time and traversed the main supply route into Fallujah in order to reach the city center. We saw artillery battery placements on the east and southeast sections of the city, along with two platoons of infantry staged to the north as we entered the city," Fulton said.

MacRae was scribbling notes on his pad. He paused, turning to the artillery battery's gunnery sergeant.

"Any issue in placing your guns or staging prior to the mission?" MacRae asked.

"As a matter of fact yes, sir," the gunnery sergeant said. "The topographical map we were using hadn't been updated in two years, and the sand dunes we were counting on for protection had shifted. It left my Marines exposed and was a challenge we didn't plan for."

MacRae made a note of it on his pad.

"And how did that effect your timeline?" he asked.

"That snafu made us a half hour late as we had to shift position and fill sandbags to create the berms we were counting on already being there," the gunnery sergeant said.

"Roger that," MacRae responded. He turned to an officer in a flight suit next to him and asked, "Air support, any pre-mission issues?"

"None to speak of," Captain Barclay said. "We had the support we needed and all ships were on time for takeoff."

MacRae noted it and turned to Fulton. He found it interesting that because the Marines had their roots in Naval warfare, they still referred to their planes and helicopters as 'ships.'

"Any pre-mission issues for the patrol itself?" he asked.

"Our go-day shifted from yesterday to today, and that caused some supply and communication issues," Fulton said. "We were staged to leave early yesterday morning, but the intelligence we received changed and we were told the mission shifted for today. It meant our vehicles were committed here and couldn't be on their regular patrol routes."

"Roger that," MacRae responded, making a note on his pad. "Any other pre-mission issues to add?"

Silence from the crowd, so MacRae continued.

"Let's talk about the ingress portion of the mission, everything from when the patrol left Camp Fallujah to its arrival at the city center," MacRae directed.

"Well, we were expecting to meet heavy resistance as we traveled through the city, including small arms fire, roadblocks, and possibly rocket attacks," Fulton said. "However, we didn't encounter any. It was as smooth sailing as we could have hoped for."

"And arty'?" MacRae asked the gunnery sergeant.

"Someone was 'hot-micing' our radio channel so we had no communication with the patrol as it entered the city," the gunnery sergeant responded.

Radio handsets had a button that was pressed when someone wished to speak. If it was accidentally depressed, it effectively blocked the radio frequency and prevented anyone from being able to communicate on that channel.

"Anything else?" MacRae asked the gunnery sergeant.

"No, sir," was the reply.

"Air support? Anything?" MacRae asked.

"Nothing to report," Captain Barclay said.

"Alright then, let's go over the patrol's arrival at the city center," MacRae said.

"We arrived ahead of our timeline, so I was coordinating with headquarters on whether we should sit tight or get the general in early. The general exited his vehicle on his own, along with his translators, so we just rolled with it. Semper Gumby," Fulton said. "It was the right thing to do because no one wanted him exposed. However, it meant we had to scramble out of our vehicles to cover his route and provide security."

MacRae nodded, scratching notes onto his clipboard.

Fulton continued, "We'd never dealt with a large crowd of military-aged males here that weren't being hostile to us, so my Marines were on edge. Things could have escalated quickly."

"Good, we'll expand on that in a minute," MacRae said. "Arty? Anything to add at this point?"

"Negative, sir," the gunnery sergeant said. "By that point, we regained communications and were standing by for any further word."

"Air support? Anything?" MacRae asked Barclay.

"We had an overflight between two of our drones when we realized so many people were concentrated on the rooftops of the surrounding buildings," Barclay said. "Our intelligence analysts were wondering what image was coming from where, but they got it sorted out. I don't think it hindered our operational capabilities."

"Anything else to add up to this point?" MacRae asked the group.

One Marine that hadn't said a word until now stepped forward and spoke up.

"Well, sir, we were having an issue with some weapons in the crowd of males across the street and in the surrounding buildings," he said.

MacRae nodded, urging the Marine to continue.

"We'd been given clear rules of engagement that said if they pointed their weapons in a hostile way, we could engage. But because their tribal leaders were in the meeting room, we weren't sure if the males were part of a security detail or whether they were looking for trouble," the Marine added.

"Understood, thanks for that," MacRae said.

"Unless anyone has anything to add, let's move onto when General Mathis was inside the city center," MacRae said.

"We had the patrol spread out into static positions, holding a security perimeter the entire time," Fulton said.

"Our overwatch flight patterns continued, and we didn't encounter anything worth mentioning," Barclay added.

"We were monitoring our radio channels, waiting for a call for fire. Nothing to report," the artillery gunnery sergeant said.

"I had something come up," one of the Marines in the back of the crowd said.

The other Marines parted to let him through. He wasn't a member of their platoon – they recognized him as one of the general's translators.

"I had an initial order to relay details about the meeting to the staff sergeant," Sgt. Lewis said to MacRae. "After that, I was under orders to aid security. We had a change of plans and I was ordered back into the meeting room to protect the general. Me going back in could have caused additional security concerns from the tribal leaders."

"Thanks, we'll circle back on that," MacRae said, noting it on his pad. "Now let's go from when the patrol left the city center and egressed out of the city itself. Staff sergeant, anything to note?"

"We did see the streets fill up pretty quickly when we left. Lots of armed males. If we had to get back in there for any reason, things could have gotten hairy," Fulton said.

"Roger, arty' and air support?" MacRae asked.

"Nothing for us, sir," the gunnery sergeant said. "We waited until the patrol passed by us and then pulled back ourselves, according to the plan."

"Very good. Air support?" MacRae asked Barclay.

"Nothing for us, either. We followed the patrol out on overwatch. We saw the streets fill up with possible civilians, possible hostiles, was hard to tell from that high up," Barclay added.

"Ok, very good then," MacRae said as he reviewed his notes. This was where the most valuable part of the after-action report came in — when they gathered lessons that could be turned into best practices.

"Let's start with your team's placement, gunnery sergeant," MacRae said. "What's your recommendation for dealing with this in the future?"

"To start with, we need more accurate topographical maps," the gunnery sergeant said. "Barring that, we need someone with eyes on the area to confirm our emplacement site provides adequate cover before we roll out there on a tight timeline."

"Got you, thanks," MacRae said. "The next issue I noted was the hot mic."

"Yeah, that couldn't have happened at a worse time," the gunnery sergeant said. "We figured out one of our sergeants had his mic caught on a piece of gear. When he didn't hear any traffic for five minutes, he picked up his radio and realized he'd been hogging the channel."

"And any advice to solve the problem in the future?" MacRae asked.

"Let's move our radio checks closer than five minutes apart during missions like this," the gunnery sergeant said. "It wasn't until seven or eight minutes into it the sergeant realized the mistake he'd made. If we establish more frequent communication, it may solve the problem. That way, if we don't hear any traffic after three minutes or so, we know to check our radios."

"Good, thanks," MacRae said. "After that, I had the patrol arriving early with the General exiting the vehicles and rushing inside. Staff sergeant, care to comment on that?"

"Yes, sir," Fulton responded. "I'd say in the future we need to brief an early-arrival protocol. We assumed that we would encounter resistance on the way in the city. When we didn't, our whole timeline slipped forward."

"Good idea," MacRae said. "And then your Marines mentioned seeing weapons in the crowd?"

"Yes, sir, we all noticed that," Fulton said. "I'd recommend a suspension of current rules of engagement in that situation so we can better assess what constitutes a hostile threat. On a normal patrol it may not be necessary, but when we are going somewhere and trying not to get in a firefight, we should change our rules of engagement."

"Thanks, I'll add that in," MacRae said. "Next, I have a change of plans from our interpreter?"

"That's right, sir," Lowis said. "Thinking about it now, I'd say that with a high-value target like the general in the room, we keep as many eyes on him as possible throughout the meeting. Me leaving could have caused more trouble than it was worth if anyone in there was nervous. And me staying would only have delayed the information I gave the staff sergeant by a few minutes."

"Thanks for that input," MacRae said. Looking over the after-action report's notes, he saw there were some solid best-practices to be learned from the mission. Surely, it wouldn't be the last time the Marines transported a high-value target into a dangerous area. The lessons they gathered here could ensure the next one was a success as well.

"Gentlemen, we're done here. As always, if anything comes to mind we didn't cover, please let me know," MacRae told the Marines.

They nodded and turned, feeling the effects of adrenaline withdrawal that normally came when they returned from a hazardous mission. As the Marines dispersed to unload and clean their vehicles and equipment, MacRae watched as they broke off into groups of friends, of comrades. The sun was beginning to leave the sky, casting shadows on the brown, sandy ground that made up the barren landscape of the camp. MacRae turned and walked toward the canvas tent that served as his office. The end of one day and the beginning of another were always special times for MacRae. It meant more missions to debrief, more lessons to be captured and more challenges to overcome.

"Always something more to learn," he said to himself as he walked over to his computer, ready to record and share the lessons the Marines shared with him.

UNITED STATES MARINE CORPS
2D BATTALION, 2D MARINES
2D MARINE DIVISION
BOX 1776
CAMP LEJEUNE, NC 29908

IN REPLY REFER TO:
1500
S-3/cbk
13 JUNE 04

From: Executive Officer
To: Commanding Officer

Subj: AFTER-ACTION REPORT (AAR) FOR THE 2D BATTALION, 2D MARINES 'DEAD MAN'S PATROL'

1. The enclosed after action comments reflect the lessons learned by the patrol team and the issues for consideration for upcoming high-value target transports in support of Operation Enduring Freedom (OEF). Information will be presented in the topic, discussion, recommendation format.

2. Topic: Artillery Battery Placement

Discussion: Artillery placement location designated during planning was not feasible in execution due to changing topographical features. The delay incurred by the artillery battery in relocating and establishing their position could have jeopardized their ability to offer artillery support to the patrol if needed.

Recommendation: It is recommended that all topographical maps be ensured for accuracy by 1) Ensuring they are no more than two years of age, and 2) Using ground intelligence to confirm placement positions are still feasible at least two days prior to the mission.

3. Topic: Communication Channel Override 'Hot Mic'

Discussion: Communication channel was rendered inoperable during critical phase of patrol ingress into hostile territory. Cause was a 'hot mic,' accidentally depressing call button.

Recommendation: It is recommended that radio checks/traffic be increased in frequency to no less than once every three minutes during high-risk phases of operations.

4. Topic: Early Arrival During High-Risk Meetings

Discussion: High-value target patrol encountered no resistance along ingress route and arrived at location prior to scheduled time. This increased the risk to both security detachment and high-value target.

Recommendation: Establish an early-arrival protocol prior to mission and brief all players in their roles.

5. Topic: Security detachment of high-value target during meetings with tribal leaders

Discussion: In a limited-security scenario, one of the security detachment exited the room to pass intelligence. Re-entry raised security concerns of tribal elders but was deemed necessary to provide adequate security of high-value target.

Recommendation: Maintain high level of security at all times during meetings with potentially hostile natives and brief intelligence once high-value targets are back in safe zone.

7. The point of contact for any issues contained in this document is the Battalion Executive Officer, Captain Jared MacRae.

J. MacRae

THE BUSINESS: PROCESS, PART II

October 23, 2015
Alpharetta, GA

J oseph MacRae picked up his office phone on the first ring because he was expecting the call. It was 5 p.m., and that meant the delivery team would be returning from their last job site of the day. The call was from the company dispatcher to let him know the large box truck had just pulled into the lot. MacRae saved the work he was doing on his computer and picked his coat up from the back of his chair. Sliding his arms into it, he was thankful it was lighter than the protective gear he had worn when deployed. Being a veteran had helped him land his job as an operations and finance manager for the largest furniture distributor in Alpharetta. However, it was what he brought to the company that had made it the most successful in Alpharetta and even nearby Atlanta, where a majority of their clients were.

Admittedly, MacRae had a lot to learn when he resigned his commission with the Marines – the civilian market couldn't understand how his job as an intelligence officer fit with their business objectives. After all, it was rare that a company needed to gather ground intelligence on their delivery routes. However, when MacRae combined his love of innovation, numbers and creating best practices, he found his fit. His only challenge was where to apply it.

It was at a family get-together that a path formed for the former captain. A younger cousin was working for a furniture distributor outside of Atlanta and was complaining about the constant rework he and his crew had to perform at job sites. Whether it was the customer changing their mind or the salesperson not mapping the office space correctly, the delivery crews were always behind schedule because of last-minute changes. When MacRae asked if the delivery teams ever got together with salespeople and management to work out a process to solve their problems, his cousin told him:

"We should, but we're too busy delivering and installing. The salespeople are too busy selling. Management is too busy, well, doing whatever it is they do."

MacRae saw the humor in that, but he also saw an opportunity.

"Surely, that company can't be as busy as we were in Iraq, sending out dozens of patrols or 'deliveries' every single day," MacRae thought to himself. "We had challenging objectives and every mission ended up changing because of our 'clients,' yet we still accomplished our objectives on time."

MacRae saw an opportunity to help the company, and perhaps his career. Convincing management that he had the solution to their problem was another matter. After a few meetings with his cousin's supervisor, MacRae was introduced to the warehouse supervisor. MacRae still remembered walking into the warehouse in the middle of a hot, humid Georgia summer. The warehouse supervisor was ensconced in his office, surrounded by delivery orders and obviously overwhelmed.

"Oh, you're my 11:30?" the warehouse supervisor asked MacRae.

"Yes, sir, that's me," he responded.

"Well, we don't have any openings on the delivery teams," the warehouse supervisor told him. "We're already using contractors because we can't predict our volume. Not enough demand to keep full-timers on and have them sitting around."

"I understand completely," MacRae said. "I wasn't thinking about working on the delivery teams, but I did have an idea about how to help them, and," MacRae motioned to the piles of delivery orders on the man's desk, " … take a lot off your plate, as well."

"Really?" the man asked, looking out over the stacks of folders. "I'm all ears."

That conversation was five years ago, and MacRae had been able to help the company grow from tenth in their industry to first, even overtaking their competitors in Atlanta to become top in their regional market. It wasn't an easy job, but as MacRae had once read, 'Every journey begins with a single step.' It was this single step, repeated again and again, that he applied to the company's operations. Starting with the delivery teams and eventually moving to the design and sales departments, MacRae had systematically captured each division's common operational practices. Then, using a type of after-action report, he had captured their best practices and solutions to their recurring challenges. These actionable lessons were then built into the company's operational policies. That solved a majority of the obvious issues the company was facing, and profits immediately improved as customers came to expect a flawless experience and referred the furniture distributor to their associates. Additionally, costs were reduced as the warehouse supervisor began implementing the feedback his delivery teams gave about how they could improve productivity.

The hardest nut for MacRae to crack was the sales team – each of them operated independently across a wide geographic region. They were rarely in the office at the same time and often saw each other as competition for a limited pool of clients and commissions. To get their attention, MacRae positioned himself as a resource to help all of them earn more commissions. When he began debriefing each salesperson every few weeks and sharing their best practices and lessons learned with the team, even the veteran salespeople began paying attention. The newest salespeople were quickest to begin implementing the action items in the reports MacRae sent to them, and when their commissions began to steadily rise, the senior salespeople caught on.

Once the organization became used to looking for ways to improve and overcome their challenges, the action items for MacRae to process began flooding in. MacRae's biggest challenge became limiting the ideas he recommended for implementation across the various departments. Just as with the after-action reports he uploaded to the Marine Corps Lessons Learned database, there was only so much any one person could implement. MacRae became an expert at recognizing which action items would be easiest to implement and yield the most results – it was these he released to the company for implementation.

Of course, his job wasn't limited to just examining his company's operations and policies. He regularly scanned industry publications and gathered intelligence on his local competition and even interviewed lost clients. Every time a sale was lost to a competitor, MacRae would contact them and find out why the sale was lost. Although price was almost always the first reason given, when MacRae dug deeper, he found reasons ranging from personality conflicts to offering the wrong product line. These lessons were built into the company's selling policies and MacRae ensured sales weren't lost for the same reasons more than once. New and repeat sales naturally increased.

Even though the delivery teams had quickly adopted the habit of improving themselves, it didn't mean everyone in company was quick to jump on the after-action wagon. Many had been in the furniture industry for decades and rightfully asked, "Who is this young fellow trying to tell me how to do my job?"

MacRae's response was the same one he would have given the senior noncommissioned officers in the Marine Corps should they have ever asked:

"I'm not here to tell you how to do your job and I'm not asking you to change how you do things – you're obviously successful. I'm here to learn how you're so successful so others can learn from you. Leadership knows you're too busy getting the job done to have time to teach everyone, so they've asked me to help in the effort."

Once people understood the role MacRae played in the company, they were more willing to share with him the key lessons they learned through often bitter experience. MacRae then synthesized the lessons into action items and shared them so people wouldn't have to be in the industry for decades to achieve a similar level of success.

At first, the leadership of the furniture company wasn't sure what to make of MacRae. They hesitated to add 15 minutes to the shifts of all their delivery teams or ask salespeople to stop selling long enough to talk with MacRae every week. However, when they saw their profits jump and their costs reduced, they knew it was in large part because of MacRae's efforts. Because he was managing the continuous improvement program, building training manuals and remained in regular contact with every line supervisor, he was quickly promoted to head of operations. MacRae had secured a position in the company, but it was these regular meetings like the one he was about to conduct that ensured he would stay there.

MacRae crossed the breezeway that separated the furniture showroom and the warehouse. As he left the air-conditioned office and stepped into the summer heat and humidity, his glasses immediately fogged. He removed them and wiped them with a handkerchief as he climbed the steps to the warehouse entrance. The delivery team was finishing with unloading the unused furniture and used boxes from the truck. They would store the extra furniture in the warehouse for resale, send it back to the manufacturer or simply hold it for the extra parts. They were drinking water from small plastic bottles, attempting to hydrate in the oven-like environment of the open bay doors. MacRae still remembered the oven-like heat and burning sun of the many after-action reports he conducted while deployed. He was thankful for at least the shade the warehouse provided. Like the patrols he debriefed, the delivery crew was used to the process and tolerant, knowing it would only last five minutes.

When MacRae first began conducting after-action reports at the end of the delivery shifts, the workers rolled their eyes at being asked to stay an extra few minutes for a meeting. It wasn't until they saw some of their long-standing complaints actually resolved by their leadership that they began to see the value in the process. Now, senior members of the delivery teams were quick to silence the newer members and contract workers if they didn't take the after-action sessions seriously. In the few years MacRae had been working with them, the crews had seen their input considered by management and often implemented. As the amount of control they felt they had over their jobs increased, so did their confidence in the after-action process. MacRae was beginning to transition who led the after-action sessions to the senior members of the team so he could focus his time on compiling the action items from across the company that were now beginning to flood into his office.

"Welcome back!" MacRae said as he shook the hands of the six delivery team members. Each of them greeted him in turn.

"As we talked about last week, Jerry is going to start leading your after-action meetings beginning this week. He's seen enough of them, and I have full confidence he'll knock it out of the park. I'll be here in case he or any of you have questions," MacRae told the assembled team. Turning to Jerry, he said, "Jerry, the floor is yours."

"Thanks, Joe," Jerry said to MacRae. "Let's start with a time check so we know how long this takes us."

Jerry looked at his watch and read the time.

"I have 5:15 in six seconds ... five ... four ... three ... two ... and time. Ok, let's start with senior folks and move down the line in no particular order."

Jerry removed a small notebook from his shirt pocket and flipped to notes from that day's delivery.

"First, let's go over what worked and what didn't work, and the reasons. I want to start with some things I could have done better. We began using iPads to track order documents last week, and we're still working some bugs out of the software," Jerry told the group.

"Now, thinking I'd be able to access all the documents from the iPad, I didn't bring hard copies with me. That held us up 20 minutes on the first job site as I had to drive back to the warehouse and get them. My action item is to confirm those documents are loaded tomorrow morning before we step off to the first job site. I'll probably bring hard copies for a few days just in case."

"Good job, Jerry," MacRae said. "What will be your first action item to record in your after-action report?"

"To check our system and make sure the delivery documents are actually accessible from the iPad before I leave for the first job site," Jerry replied as he began writing the item in his notebook.

"Right. And how long will that action item be in effect?" MacRae asked Jerry.

"At least a week, until we're sure the bugs have been worked out of the software."

"Great," MacRae said. "Please carry on."

"Right, so the next step is for you all to give me some feedback on things I could have done better," Jerry told his team.

The first team member to speak had almost as much time in the industry as Jerry. He opened the round by saying, "Aside from the missing paperwork, I think you could have planned our route better. We lost time by staying off the interstate."

"That's good, but we need something more concrete to be able to capture an action item," MacRae said. "What's something we could do to ensure we maximize our efficiency when traveling between job sites?"

The team member thought for a second, then looked at Jerry and said, "We could pow-wow either at the beginning of the day when we get our final list of deliveries or when we're departing from one job site. Then we could talk about the best route to take."

"Awesome, we'll begin doing that tomorrow," Jerry told his crew as he wrote the item into his notebook. "Anyone have anything else?"

Another team member, one of the junior members of the crew, seeing

Jerry had the confidence to call himself out on his mistakes, said, "We had to install a corner unit in that third job site and the assembly instructions were for a different unit. When I asked you what to do, you told me to read the instructions and walked away. I had to find another team member to help me figure it out."

"I apologize for that, I didn't mean to be curt with you," Jerry told the junior team member. "The client told me she needed some last-minute changes and I was running around trying to help her, but I understand how my behavior came across to you."

He continued, "I'll take the hit on that one. In the future, I'll check to make sure we have the correct installation paperwork in case that comes up and we don't have another team member available to help out."

Jerry finished writing this latest point into his notebook, then turned to his team.

"Anything else?" he asked them.

Hearing silence, he continued, "OK, our objective today was to complete four office furniture installations during our shift and ensure our customers were 100% satisfied with our work before leaving the job sites. I think we accomplished that. Anyone have anything different?"

The team members shook their heads back and forth.

"OK, so let's look at what worked," Jerry began. "Our first job site was at Lionshare Marketing. We arrived on time, but as I mentioned, I had to double-back to the warehouse to get the paperwork. I think we did well as a team because we were able to unload the boxes and at least stage them in the rooms and begin prepping while I was on the road."

"We left that job site a few minutes behind schedule because of the paperwork issue. I think we did a good job of cleaning up and leaving the place cleaner than we found it. Does anyone have anything to add?" Jerry asked.

One of the crew members said, "We did well, but I noticed something out of the ordinary for us. We let the folks at the client site around our install areas know we would be there for a few minutes. I saw a few of their folks get up and go to another room for client calls. Letting them know we would be there was a good idea."

"Great call," Jerry said. "Why do you think we did that?"

"Well," the crew member thought, "It seemed like the right thing to do because we noticed everyone there was busy on phones and although we aren't loud, our drills can cause a racket."

"Ok, so why did we make the choice to tell them we would be working in their area?" Jerry asked again.

It was another crew member who answered him this time.

"Because we have a policy of clients being 100% satisfied with our work," she began. "That doesn't just include the furniture we install, it includes how we do our work as well."

"Right," Jerry said. "And that's valuable. What's an action item we could learn from that experience to build into how we do business in the future?"

"To appoint someone, maybe the lead on the delivery team, to notify employees in the surrounding areas of our install sites that we'll be working there for a few minutes," the crew member answered.

Jerry scribbled the idea into his notebook and asked, "Anyone have anything else from the first install today?"

When he didn't hear anything else, he continued.

"Our second site was Rock and Water Architecture. We arrived a few minutes behind schedule but were able to make up for lost time and get ourselves back on schedule. Anyone have anything from that site?"

When the crew didn't answer, MacRae prodded them with a question.

"Did everything on that job site go exactly as planned?"

"Not exactly," a crew member replied. "The doors to the building were a little tight for the desk and partitions we were installing. They were 12 feet tall, but only a little wider than a regular doorway."

"Thanks for bringing that up," Jerry said. "I saw some concern on the client's face when they saw us trying to squeeze their furniture through the doorframe. And this isn't the first time we've had to deal with a client's entrance being smaller than the boxes we were trying to move in. How have we dealt with that in the past?"

One of the senior team members responded, "Well, usually we don't notice it until we get the box to the doorway. At that point, we either ask for another entrance or break open the box and hand carry the individual pieces into the client site."

"I've seen that a few times myself," Jerry said. "And while we always deal with it, I think we can get tighter on that process. How about, in the future, the senior team member estimates the size of the boxes or measures them when we arrive on site? Then we can also measure the doorway as we enter the building to meet the client. That way, we would know if the boxes will fit or that we have to break open the box and carry the pieces in. It's always easier to break open a box close to the truck so we don't have to make another trip carrying cardboard back."

Hearing no objection to this, he wrote this next action item into his notebook and continued.

"Anyone have anything else from the second job site today?"

The team didn't have anything, so Jerry went on to the next job site.

"After we broke for lunch, we drove over to our third site, our largest job of the day, at Oakmont Accounting. We left site number two on time, but got stuck in traffic on the way over and just barely made it to the next site on time. While we didn't break our word with the client about our arrival time, it was a little too close for comfort. We have a reputation for being on time to maintain, after all."

It was the most junior crew member who spoke up next.

"This may not apply because it's something we did at my last job in trucking, but I'll offer it if you want me to."

"Of course, let's hear it!" Jerry said.

"Well, at my old job we had to be exactly on time with deliveries. If we were early, we had to sit and wait to get grocery stores to unload the produce we were carrying. If we were late, they would refuse to take the shipment altogether. To make sure we were on time, we used to drive to the next delivery site and have lunch there. Even if we got lost or were stuck in traffic, at least the grocery store wouldn't refuse shipment."

"That's a great idea!" Jerry said. "It may mean that lunch gets cut short, but as it's a paid lunch break, I think I can at least ask management about making up for the lost time at the end of the week."

He wrote down the action item in his notebook and then continued.

"Even though we had a lot to unload and install at the third client site, I thought we did a good job," Jerry said. "We were installing in an unoccupied space so we had free run of the place. And we had the iPads working by that point so we were able to walk the client through the layout of the space before we even started unloading boxes. Anyone have anything to add for that job?"

Again, he was met with silence from his crew. MacRae saw the opportunity to target their success instead of always focusing on a problem.

"So the job went great, and that was due to the great work everyone on the team did," he told the assembled crew. "So I want to know, 'Why?'"

"Well," one of the team members said, "We followed policy. As Jerry was meeting with the client, the rest of us began unloading the boxes from the truck. And as soon as we knew where the furniture was going in the building, we got it there and began assembling it."

"So your success was due to following policy?" MacRae asked.

"That's right," the team answered together.

"We had a junior team member with you today, right?" MacRae said.

"We sure did," Jerry responded. "And she did great."

"Then I want to know how a junior team member was able to integrate so quickly with the senior team members and perform at such a high capacity," MacRae asked.

It was the junior team member who responded.

"The training I had was pretty detailed," she said. "I liked how I was taught how to get everything done in the warehouse before I was ever sent to a client site. That way I didn't get nervous when we were on a time schedule. I knew exactly what role I would play and what I would be responsible for when I was finally sent out with the team to deliver and install."

"And what about the training, specifically, made you successful today?" MacRae asked. "Was it the detail, the time you spent practicing, the feedback the team gave you … ?"

"It was a little bit of all that," she answered. "But I think more than anything else, it was that I was able to demonstrate I could read the schematics of the furniture assembly before I was sent to a room by myself on a client site to assemble anything. It means I have a lot of confidence I can assemble most of what we deliver, and I can always ask a senior person if I need help."

"So what I'm hearing is," MacRae added, "the way you were trained is what made you so successful after only two weeks with the company?"

"That's right," she said.

Jerry took MacRae's cue and wrote the feedback down in his notebook. He turned to his crew and asked, "Anything else anyone wants to add about the third job today?"

After waiting a few moments, he continued.

"Alright, so I have in my notes that we left the third job site on schedule and arrived to our last job on time. That was at …" Jerry checked his notes, "Martini Savings and Loan. I have that we were slowed down a little by needing to run some wiring for electricity that we needed for the desks. That pushed us a little past five p.m. for our departure. In my book, that's a hit because we told the client we would be done by five so they could go home on time."

"But that's not your fault, is it?" MacRae chided Jerry.

"We aren't responsible for where a building has electricity wired, but we are responsible for keeping our word to our clients," Jerry answered. Looking at his crew, he asked, "So what happened, and how did we deal with it?"

It was his senior delivery person who answered.

"I've had this come up a few times at job sites," he said. "We try to pull schematics of the building before we get on site, but sometimes the schematics are wrong. In this case, the outlet we needed to run power to was a clear three feet away from the nearest desk and the client didn't want the layout rearranged. We'd never just run an extension cord from a series of desks to the wall because that looks sloppy."

"I agree, and I'm glad you upheld a high standard. That's a win in my book," Jerry said. "So how did we fix the problem?"

"Thankfully, we had the materials on the truck in a matching color to the desks we were installing to cover the extension cord and mount a protective cover over it. That allowed us to run power and have it look like part of the furniture," the senior crew member said.

"So we succeeded in preventing what could have been a re-visit to the client site. Why did we run into that situation in the first place?" Jerry asked.

"Incorrect building schematics," one crew member said.

"No one did a pre-install site visit to measure," another added.

"Both of those are right answers, and there's not a lot we can do about incorrect wiring schematics. I want to know why we didn't do a pre-install site visit."

This had been a touchy subject for some time among the delivery crews. For one, it was costly to send someone out to a client site to measure the space, and even then, the client often wanted the furniture rearranged once they saw it assembled in their offices.

"I know we can't always send someone from our delivery crew ahead to ensure the next site is good to go," Jerry said. "So what are our other options?"

"We need accurate layouts of the rooms we're going to be installing furniture in, especially when we need to run electricity to multiple units," one crew member said.

"I agree," Jerry said. "So knowing we can't send one of our people and the schematics aren't always accurate, what are our options?"

The crew was silent, and again MacRae prodded them.

"Who always visits the client site from our company?" he asked them.

"The salesperson!" they responded together.

"Couldn't the salesperson snap a few pics of the room before we leave the warehouse so we know if we need to bring any additional equipment?" MacRae asked.

"I don't see why not," said Jerry.

"Salespeople aren't installers, so they may not know what to ensure they're capturing," MacRae said. "What do you need them to make sure they take pictures of?"

One of the senior members spoke up and answered, "The layout of the room we're going to be installing in, especially the locations of the electrical outlets."

"That's right," Jerry added. "And to make sure we get it from different angles with a tape measure or ruler on the floor so we can estimate the length of any extra materials we're bringing."

"Great idea, but what motivation is a salesperson who works on straight commission going to have for doing this extra work?" MacRae asked.

In the Marines, it was expected everyone would work for the benefit of the team. He had learned that in the world of business, it was often helpful to have a motivator to get people to add tasks to their plates.

"They're paid on a percentage of the margin from the entire sale, including overall delivery costs, right?" Jerry asked MacRae.

"That's right," MacRae said.

"That last job today took us a full twenty minutes longer than it would have if we had known about the electrical layout," Jerry said. "That adds to delivery costs, which reduces our overall margin on the sale. I can work up a percentage of what 20 minutes compounded across five or six jobs each week would be to an average commission. If losing a chunk of their commission isn't enough to get them to spend three minutes taking pictures of the client site, I don't know what will be."

"A fine plan," MacRae said, "And one I think the salespeople will support when you explain how it will improve their commissions."

Jerry made a note of the action item in his notebook and continued.

"We left our last job a little late, but the client was happy with the work. They even complemented us on our efficiency in getting everything assembled and how clean the site was when we left," Jerry told his crew. "Anyone have anything else to add?"

The team shook their heads.

"Ok then, that's it for today," Jerry said. "I need my senior crew members to hang behind and prep anything we have for delivery tomorrow so we can get a good start."

Each person on the delivery shift dispersed. Some went to clock out and others to check tomorrow's orders. They would then pull the boxes that had arrived that day to the bay doors of the warehouse so they could be easily loaded the next day. Jerry and MacRae walked to the exit door of the warehouse.

"Great job, Jerry," MacRae told the delivery team supervisor. "Any questions about the after-action process? You'll be running them on your own next week."

"I don't think so," Jerry answered. "I've seen the format you need the action items in, so I'll just use that as a template. I do have a question, though."

"Yes?" MacRae asked.

"I have about four or five action items to submit in here," Jerry said, holding up his notebook. "Which ones will we have to incorporate into policy?"

"Great question," MacRae said. "A lot of times, we have great ideas that aren't financially feasible to implement right away. For instance, it took us six months to make a case for the iPads."

"I remember that," Jerry said. "But man, are they helpful!"

"I know," MacRae added. "I present all of the top-line action items or the recurring second-line ones to management each week, and we collectively decide which ones to implement. The ones that just affect your department are fairly easy as long as we have the resources to enact them. One of the challenges of conducting these After-Action Reports is defining when the changes will occur. Because we have to get approval on some of them, the timeline isn't always available."

"That includes the action items that cross over into other departments, like having salespeople take photos of job sites?"

"Right, those are trickier still," MacRae told him. "We have to get buy-in from the VP of sales. Remember, a key part of this process is communicating who will benefit from the change to policy. When you send me the numbers on percent of lost margin for having to add time at a job site, it will make it a lot easier to sell the sales department on it."

"Then I'll make sure I make a good case for it!" Jerry said. He thought a minute and then added, "You know, in other jobs I've had, we usually had to wait until someone retired to make changes, and then a lot would change at once, not always for the good. Then things wouldn't change again for a long time."

"Yes, I know what you mean," MacRae said.

"Yeah, but here," Jerry added, "It seems like we're always looking for better ways to get things done. I know that's played a part in making us the best at what we do in Alpharetta, even Atlanta. But I'm wondering if we'll ever get to a place where there's nothing left to improve, no more changes to be made to make us better?"

MacRae answered, "Not on my watch."

PART II:
Field Guide

FIELD GUIDE: PIVOT POINT

Any good field guide will not only tell you how to accomplish something, but it will also include the why. Because this field guide includes both the strategy and execution of your objectives, knowing how to get buy-in from your team is just as important as how you implement your plan. As you move forward in creating a Pivot Point in your organization, it's vital you understand why the process is so powerful, and that starts with understanding what it is and what it isn't.

What It Isn't

Modern managers are inundated with requests – most from the demands of running the day-to-day operations of their business. In the midst of this, they are expected to learn and apply new leadership techniques, planning processes, and engagement programs. Many would freely admit this is one of the things that falls to the lower end of the priority list. After all, as many experienced business owners will often state, 'No revenue, no business.'

Precisely because leaders at all level of business are overloaded with demands, they need something that doesn't create more work for them and their people. If anything, they need a process that reduces the many tasks they're responsible for delivering *in addition to helping them overcome unforeseen changes in their plans.* The foundational need behind why the military developed the elements of Pivot Point is because they needed something that would allow people to perform consistently in a fast-paced, constantly-changing environment full of challenges. As anyone who works in emergency services or the military can attest, in a world where mistakes mean life and death, there isn't time for anything else. In the same way, business leaders know recurring errors and a culture of 'winging it' means the life (and eventually, death) of their organization. They recognize last-minute changes are inevitable and need a way to reduce or eliminate these changes' effects on results. A high-performance culture needs something that will reduce the mental load on their people, not increase it.

The process you'll learn in the following pages is not a management 'technique,' although it certainly includes many aspects of project management. Additionally, it's not a 'leadership method,' although it does point to the traits that have guided leaders to some incredible wins. Most importantly, a Pivot Point isn't a band aid to fix a broken company. However, it is a way to save and improve it.

Pivot Points can exist in many places throughout an organization, from the executive suite down to the people responsible for delivering value to customers. It can also be the underpinning process that a company uses to drive all of its operations in a way that sets any strategy up for the greatest odds for success. Whether that project is strategic innovation or simply adding a few pennies to your margin, creating a Pivot Point allows organizations to perform to the best of their ability and continuously improve. For these reasons, Pivot Point is best used as the shared planning and operational model inside an organization. It should serve as the bridge that links departments together. However, if you're like many organizations, you don't use a consistent planning model across operations at all – a challenge whose remedy we will now address.

How does one go about introducing Pivot Point into an organization? There are two ways that set you up for the greatest success, depending on whether you lead multiple teams – in which case your title may be CEO,

COO, CMO, operations manager or something similar – or whether you are running a small team/single project and you want to get started at your current level.

If you are in the former category, managing multiple teams and responsible for multi-phase projects, then the best way to introduce a Pivot Point into your organization is from the beginning of your next strategic, multi-team planning session. It is there people will be most receptive to the idea of actually planning, in detail, how you will overcome the last-minute changes that often hinder or derail projects. Additionally, the buy-in of senior leadership and the cascading business objectives that will come from these planning meetings will be much more successful if each of them is fractal. In this way, all your business objectives, no matter their size, are planned and executed using the same system. This will make your continuous improvement process powerful and part of a culture that welcomes change. We'll discuss that in the section about the fourth P: Process.

Most importantly, introducing Pivot Point during your planning sessions will allow you to address the many unforeseen changes that normally derail business objectives as your people are in the field executing your plans.

However, if you are in the latter camp and are leading a team of ten or less people, or just focused on a single 'can't fail' project, create a Pivot Point around its planning, preparing, performing and processing. You'll have a much greater chance of your project succeeding, and when your coworkers realize you're using a consistent and repeatable process to drive results, they'll want to know how you did it.

Whether you're in leadership or leading a team of one, it's never too late to begin using the process you'll learn in the following pages to set yourself – and your business objectives – up for success. You can start at the strategy level of an organization or at the bottom where the rubber meets the road. Because Pivot Point was designed to serve the top and bottom echelons of an organization, it will serve you no matter where you are on the ladder.

The Four P's of Pivot Point

So what, exactly, are the Four P's of Pivot Point, and how do I use them in my organization or on my team to deal with the challenges that so often get in the way? The Four P's are centered around four basic concepts, the same concepts you read about in the stories of the 'Dead Man's Patrol' and through the narratives of how those same skills were applied in the business world. Each was designed to mitigate or eliminate the effects of unexpected changes to your plans. Those basic concepts are Planning, Preparing, Performing and Processing. I'll explain their roots in the following sections, so you understand why they're important.

THE *WHY* OF THE FOUR P'S

<u>Planning</u>

When I first set foot on the battlefield, I was surprised that so many moving pieces could come together for a singular purpose. Assets from the air, land and sea were all coordinated to execute their objectives on a timeline that didn't allow for tardiness. Of course, for a 19-year old in that scenario, everything is impressive. As my months rolled into years spent with combat units, I became less impressed with the vehicles, ships and planes they could summon and became more impressed with the work that went into arranging them. There was a lot riding on their missions being successful and still somehow finding a way of bringing everyone home at the end of the day. As I began to attend planning sessions, I saw a unique process at work – one that addressed all the changes that normally stop a plan in its tracks. It was a method that ensured a maximum rate of return, not in dividends but in raw results.

In the *Marine Corps Warfighting Publication (MCWP) 5-1, Marine Corps Planning Process*, Marine Corps leaders are instructed exactly how to plan for their operations. They're instructed to look at the totality of their objective – everything from why they're trying to accomplish what they're doing, to where and when it must be done, and exactly who will accomplish what.

Before any of us stepped out the gate onto a patrol, even before we

141

visited our families on leave, the challenges we might face were considered by our leaders. While most enlisted troops never see behind the curtain of this planning process, they feel its effects. I witnessed these affects as a young lance corporal – billions of dollars of assets coordinated to achieve a single objective. Of course, our planners were professionals of top caliber. The military invests a lot of money in its war colleges attended by senior officers – many are on par with Ivy League schools. By the time they were allowed to actively lead planning sessions for the missions Marines like me were executing, even our new leaders had 'decades' of experience. What made them different from the 'veteran' employees in your organization? These officers had been trained how to gather the experiences of their peers through the Marine Corps Lesson Learned Program (addressed later in this section) as they were rising in the ranks. They were also trained to share their experience with the organization when called upon. This feedback loop ensured the variables that reduced performance were accounted for and dealt with before people's lives (or your organization's resources) were risked.

This allows the military to do something large organizations will be clamoring for in the next decade – transitioning the knowledge of their experienced baby boomers to the millennial generation who will be replacing them before 2020. Unlike what most businesses do today, each of our missions wasn't just planned from looking at 'what we're going to do' and 'what's available to get the job done'. Of course, those are the foundations of planning and we definitely used them. But that's only half of the puzzle. An integral part of our planning process involved planning our missions from looking at 'what changes did we encounter in past missions' and 'how would we want to have done it differently?' Those two critical questions are an important and often overlooked part of ensuring experience is brought to bear on a plan. Additionally, those two questions begin the transfer of knowledge from one generation to another.

Once our planning sessions reached this point, it was a fair bet separate roles would be assigned to ensure it was executed. Most organizations are adept enough at project management to realize someone has to be accountable for specific results, but that's not enough. Knowing who is responsible for delivering a result doesn't ensure they'll produce the result you want. In a well-known management parable, a manager asks one of his people to plan a company picnic. The employee, believing they were doing a great job, went out and bought the ingredients for grilling: hot dogs, beef patties, veggie burgers, etc. The day of the picnic, the CEO inspects the preparations and becomes furious – in his mind, he saw a country club gala. Not knowing this, his employee delivered something more akin to a family reunion barbecue. The key error in the story – and in most company's accountability processes – was one thing: not communicating expectations.

In the military, we've learned that we have to be very specific in issuing objectives. A belief exists among Marine non-commissioned officers that if they tell their junior Marines to destroy something, they better make sure to account for the forests, buildings, or anything else that should still be standing after the mission. Having seen the passion and destructive force of a group of heavily-armed 18-21 year olds myself, I think the belief is well-founded. As a result of coming up in the ranks, leaders are very specific with what the end-state of each result will look like. This changes 'Capture Target A' to 'Capture Target A And Minimize Collateral Damage.'

Where most organizations drop the ball is clearly defining the expected outcomes of each of the courses of action they assign to individual team members. Whether we're miscommunicating our timelines or our desired outcomes, the result is the same. It threatens the success of your business objectives and ultimately your organization's future, and leaves a massive hole where unexpected change will creep in. For this reason, make your courses of action crystal clear to each person responsible for delivering on it. It's impossible to deal with unexpected change when no one understand what the end-state of the project should look like.

The final stage of planning in the military is when we ask a very important question: What changes and challenges **haven't we planned for**? This question reveals any gaps we may have missed in the other stages of planning and is the single biggest factor in preparing for the unexpected things that normally derail our objectives.

Before a patrol steps out the gate to protect a bridge while a convoy crosses, they want to know what they're supposed to do if they convoy is late. They want to know what to do if it gets dark and they're running out of night-vision batteries. Why do they want to know all of these things before they leave the comfort of their forward operating base? Because being stuck on a bridge among a heavily-armed population when darkness comes is not the time to count on rational thought. To prevent mistakes from being made, the military always asks 'what could go wrong' before it goes wrong. This ensures they have a better chance of things going right.

<u>Preparing</u>

A routine every enlisted person who ever served in the modern military is familiar with is the 'pre-mission brief.' In the Marine Corps and in other branches, this is known by the acronym SMEAC. It stands for 'Situation,' 'Mission,' 'Execution,' 'Administration' and 'Command and Signals.' While there is a SMEAC-style 'brief' for everything in the military from maintaining nuclear launch codes to drinking and driving while on leave, everyone understands and appreciates its value. Whether it was to re-confirm the mission objective hadn't changed or to ensure everyone understood what they would be responsible for doing, the pre-mission brief served a critical function among troops. It aligns them to a common goal and allows for innovation. The value of alignment is known in the business world and in the military, but is often overlooked as something secondary to revenue. The military knows that when achieving results, alignment isn't a 'nice to have' – it's a necessity. Because a combat environment can change in a second, it is vital that people be able to innovate new ways to achieve their objective. In an ever-changing market, businesses need people with the ability to come up with faster, better ways of dealing with last-minute changes. The military proves that this is not a character trait, but rather a methodology. That's what preparing is all about: confirming that people know what their end-state is and what they have available to achieve it.

Alignment and innovation are also key benefits of having a Pivot Point in your organization.

Performing

Any service member can tell you that most of their time serving their country was not spent on the battlefield, but rather in training. Training is a critical element of standardizing performance. It's why the military is willing to invest close to a hundred thousand dollars in training even employees in 'non-technical' fields. It's easy to spend money on education, just ask any parent subsidizing college or paying private-school tuition. The question is: What kind of training makes people most-able to perform under stress and task overload, most able to pivot when the unexpected inevitably occurs? There are PhD programs that scratch the surface of that question, but I can share what I saw from people who were responsible for delivering results in the most challenging environments on the planet. The military's training process is a simple, two-step process – Demo, Do. The process was simple because the military invested time in gathering the wisdom of their senior leaders. Additionally, junior members are usually trained by senior people in their same career field who have recently rotated in from performing the same task they'll be training.

This stands in contrast to the training programs of many organizations. The majority of them are either incomplete or nonexistent. Those who have a training department often have individuals teaching and assessing skills they themselves never had to perform.

Of course, in the military, as in business, the success and failure of training does not fall squarely on the shoulders of instructors. Rather, the military places most of the responsibility for success on the shoulders of the trainees. For modern troops, each opportunity to advance in their fields is seen as a privilege, even if it doesn't come with a raise. As a result, military students are dedicated to learning new skills from their instructors.

Performance in a training environment and performance in the field or a client-facing position can yield entirely different results. How someone operates under the stress of timetables, pressure to succeed and having revenue on the line can be different from how they perform in a testing environment. To ensure people can perform where it's needed most, the best instructors know that's where they need to assess their students – in an environment as realistic as they can make it, and sometimes even more stressful than the one they'll be performing in. If one of their students can perform to a high standard there, instructors have confidence they will be able to perform anywhere.

Performance doesn't stop with one's own duties when they're part of a team. In environments where people have to play multiple roles at key moments to achieve an objective, performance becomes even more important. As technology continues to change the way we do business, we can all rest assured our jobs will only become more complicated – not less. That means if people don't know how to manage multiple priorities simultaneously, they'll be overtaken by competitors that can.

Space is at a premium on the battlefield. Of course, the more people we have, the more chances we have of succeeding. However, we can only carry so many people on a patrol. The military handles this challenge through training not just the skills of someone's primary positons, but also ensures they know how to pick up elements of their teammate's roles when needed. A perfect example of this is when a group goes into a house to ensure it is free of threats. The lead person constantly changes as one member of the squad enters a room and the others continue to search the house. In the business realm, every team has an opportunity to improve their effectiveness by understanding not only their specific and specialized role, but also how to support the team when their specialized role isn't required.

Adapting this skillset in an organization means a force multiplier for teams that embrace it. Not only is it useful when someone is unexpectedly called away, it also ensures everyone's actions are aligned to achieving critical objectives. As a leader, you can ensure that when your employees are not being specialists in their individual roles, they can at least be generalists at increasing your bottom line.

Processing

Looking at results is nothing new for most organizations. Whether it's a shareholder report or a CFO's brief, organizations need to track their results. Unfortunately, few ever take the time to consider 'why did that negative result happen?' Even fewer ask the more valuable question, 'how did we get the result we were aiming for (or exceed it)?'

In the Marine Corps, the process was valuable enough to be established as an official program by *Marine Corps Order 3504.1*. While your organization won't be placing heavy artillery, you will want to know how to learn from the challenges you've overcome – something most organizations never take the time to do.

That's the reason most organizations are struggling to innovate, struggling to share a repeatable system their teams can use to deal with last-minute changes to their plans. They don't take the time to ask the right questions. When success is a matter of life and death, as it is on the battlefield, these are questions that we can't afford not to ask. As last-minute changes inevitably occur, service members need to know there's a plan in place to deal with them. The lessons that build those contingency plans comes from after-action reports.

Because after-action reports are a proven asset for success in the military, it's surprising how little they are used in other industries. There is a stigma around the process most companies share, and it is largely due to the name businesses give this process – 'Post-Mortems.' The name alone is enough to turn people off to using it as part of their culture. As a business leader, it's vital to consider how to introduce after-action reports into your organization. You want your peers and leadership to see the value in examining not only your failures, but your successes as well.

I learned this particular lesson not from someone I met on the battlefield, but in the boardroom. A former executive with IBM, this gentleman explained to me that when his sales teams used post-mortems after they lost sales, people always learned something, but they were only learning what not to do. One day, someone on his review team had the nerve to ask, "Why are we only looking at our failures? What if we began looking at our successes too? Then we're know how to replicate success instead of avoiding failure." Of course, sales increased for them.

Same process, different solutions.

That's why, if you're getting ready to launch after-action reports into your organization, it's usually best to start with a success. That gets people aligned and immediately seeing the value in looking at what happened.

Using the Four P's in Your Organization

You've read about the elements of Pivot Point in action on the battlefield and in business. We've reviewed why creating a Pivot Point made the men and women I studied so successful. Now it's time to look at using it to rapidly increase your chances of success when change is a constant of life. And change is something we all must deal with – the question is: how? At its root, using a Pivot Point in your organization is establishing an insurance policy against the effects of the one constant you have – unforeseen challenges. Because this process helps users to identify resources, assesses risk and align employees before change derails your objectives, changes to your plan can be mitigated. They can't be stopped, but we can prepare a plan to deal with them.

With all the changes that a business could face and the limited time many leaders have, it makes sense they would want to try and establish elements of Pivot Point somewhere in their organization. There will always be some areas that need more attention than others. However, it's important to understand what makes this system successful on the battlefield also makes it successful in business. It isn't solely through clear objectives or learning from mistakes. It comes from integrating a comprehensive planning and execution process into all of our operations. Let's examine some of the most common questions I hear from leaders who only want to implement certain elements of Pivot Point, and my response:

I see a need for clear business objectives. But as a leader, I'm not currently preparing line workers, having them perform multiple-role tasks, or capturing lessons at the end of projects. Can't I just use the planning process and be more successful with clear objectives?

Of course, just using the planning process outlined here will put you above 99% of your competition by the very fact that so few people take the time to comprehensively plan to that level of detail. However, planning is not the only reason Pivot Point works so well in business. Unless you are part of one of the few industries that are not experiencing drastic change – either through governmental regulation, new competition, market shifts or changing customer needs – then your plans will change as you execute them. When they do, all the great planning documents you and your leadership team made will end up on the bottom of birdcages. In the 18th century, a German field marshal said that no plan survives contact with the enemy. No plan in your business will last past the first change your customer, supplier, internal team, or regulatory agency throws your way. Having an airtight plan helps in mitigating this, but it's your folks' ability to enact their standards and protocols, continually align on the changing goal and finally process the event that will ensure their continued success into the future. That begins with the planning process, but doesn't end with it.

There is a big need to get my folks aligned, and preparing my folks each day makes sense, but they're just line workers. None of them are involved in planning, perform multiple roles or do 'after-actions' on their work. Can't I just prepare/align my team and leave it at that?

While it is good for leaders to want to align their employees around a common goal, many feel that their employees already have a good handle on their roles and what is expected of them. Therefore, they don't participate in planning, and, like most organizations, don't do 'after-actions.' If yours is the rare business where everything remains static through an entire year, quarter, week, day and shift, then a basic check-in may be all you need. However, after having worked with companies from mom-and-pop startups to Fortune 100 global enterprises, not once have I seen an entire execution cycle remain exactly the same as when it was dreamed up in the planning room. Whether we like it or not, we are living in an ever-changing world, where we are beholden to the demands of multiple stakeholders. Because of that, something in your plan will change from inception to execution. If you prepare your people from a plan that is no longer accurate and up-to-date, then they'll be executing on outdated objectives. For that reason, the military involves many levels of command in their planning sessions. Everyone gets prepared before they execute, high performance is achieved through constant updates against an inevitably moving target, and after-actions are applied to update their mission objectives. In the same way, your organization needs to account for the fact that business objectives will likely shift at least slightly between planning, execution and delivery of your product or service. To not include the planning, performing and processing stages of the model means the results your teams achieve may not be in the best interest of your business.

I need my people to perform well, but management already has a semi-decent planning process. They do the same thing every day, so we don't need any preparation, and we're too busy to process our results anyway.

There's no arguing that the most important thing your folks do is perform their roles well — that's what generates the revenue that keeps you in business, after all. Therefore, it makes sense to invest resources in making sure your folks are safe, efficient, and turn out a quality product or service with minimal errors. Many companies have built their brands on an outstanding product or service. Unfortunately, just being concerned with performance leaves massive holes in your strategy — holes that your competition will be all too happy to exploit. And holes where unexpected change will creep in to derail your objectives. If your teams are not actively engaged in planning how they will achieve their objectives, it will be difficult to gain their buy-in. If you're not preparing them each day by updating them on your environment's changing needs, they may execute against the wrong objectives. Finally, if you are not learning from your stellar results through processing your performance, then you will continue to perform at your current level. Your competition, on the other hand, is always looking for a way to surpass your results. If you involve all the aspects of Pivot Point within a well-performing team, you ensure their ability to exponentially improve performance.

We have a great planning process already. Our folks are all experienced so we don't need to prepare. They're already performing at a high level; we just need to process better. Can we just do after-action reports?

Of all the Ps of Pivot Point, the most underutilized and perhaps the most powerful is processing, so congrats on seeing where your time can have the greatest impact. However, there is a fundamental flaw in attempting to process a daily shift's work, execution cycle or business objective without bringing in the other elements of Pivot Point. First, with no clear objective, what will you process against? Profitability? You may have made money, but you'll never know if you should have made more. Secondly, with no preparation, how can you ensure all your folks were on the same page when they were executing? Third, if you never established accountable actions in your planning, preparation and performance, how will you know where training can be improved? Processing is immensely valuable, but to build the structure that allows for processing to be effective, you need to ensure each of the elements of Pivot Point are brought to bear.

HOW TO USE THE FOUR P'S

Now that you understand where the elements of Pivot Point came from and the importance of using Plan, Prepare, Perform and Process as a comprehensive operational system, let's look at how to incorporate each of the Ps of Pivot Point into your organization. We'll now explore how to use this powerful tool to achieve your business objectives and continually improve your results.

Plan – Precise, Profitable and In Line With Your Purpose

Most organizations have some form of planning process, whether they realize it or not. As I watched how business leaders planned, I noticed one similarity – each planning method was unique to the person, the team and the organization. That is actually a good thing! However, as is often the case in military strategy, one's greatest strength is often their greatest flaw. The drawback to a planning process that is unique to the individual leader, team and organization is by definition the process can't be replicated. As we've already seen, a process that can't be scaled and replicated leaves itself vulnerable to the inevitable changes organizations encounter.

The other side of the coin is a strictly regimented planning process that does not take into account unique features of an organization's organic culture, customer expectations, or quality control processes. Obviously, a planning process that isn't adapted to your planning session's needs, whether strategic (long-range) or tactical (short-range) is likely to cause more harm than good.

So what's the ideal solution? What's a planning process that will work equally well whether we are using it for long-range strategy involving thousands of individuals across multiple continents or for a short-term goal involving a small team? Not only that, but a process that works well across multiple industries that can be tailored to meet the unique needs of that organization? Can such a process exist?

I believe it can, because I've seen it successfully used in both strategic and tactical planning, across multiple organizations with sometimes opposite cultures and conflicting objectives. The value of this planning process is that it isn't regimented. Therefore, by its very nature, it has to be used in the context of the organization's unique values, business objectives and capabilities where it is applied.

In the military, plans have to meet three qualifications – they have to be precise, they have to move the campaign forward (be profitable), and they have to be in line with the organization's purpose. It doesn't sound complicated, and it isn't. However, it is detailed enough to ensure it is worth pursuing. Additionally, its structure serves as the first line of defense against unexpected change. When planning business objectives, your objective also has to be precise, profitable and in line with the organization's purpose.

Precise

What is a precise plan?

Firstly, it's tied to a specific completion date. Why is this important? If your plan doesn't have a 'due date,' one of two things will happen: your team(s) will miss your deadline, mucking up your objectives' timelines and costing revenue; or, perhaps worse, they'll rush in the final hours to achieve their objective while sacrificing quality and standards. In either of those cases, your organization will be struggling to deal with errors caused by rushed work and rework. Surprisingly, this simple method is often ignored when business leaders are planning. Often, they'll assign a vague timeline – such as 'by the end of second quarter' – or ignore a timeline altogether. Unfortunately, not attaching a specific date to your objective's completion means you can't coordinate multiple objectives on a timeline. You also can't build in the necessary time to deal with changes that will inevitably arise as your folks work to reach your goals.

Secondly, a plan is tied to an extremely precise end-state. Remember when I said that Marines have learned to be very specific about the results they want their troops to achieve? This is because they know if they tell Marines to capture an objective on the other side of the mountain, they had better let them know the mountain should remain intact. While your teams may not have the willpower – or the firepower – to level a mountain, they do have the power to give you an entirely different result than the one you were expecting. Because the precision of your goals matter just as much as their timelines, ensure that you're creating objectives that have tangible outcomes. Whether that is a report or a piece of software, make sure that everyone understands exactly what is expected. Combine that precise *what* with a specific *when*, and you'll know your folks are halfway to mitigating any change that might occur.

Bad Example Of A Business Objective:

Increase bottom-line profits in second quarter.

Pivot Point Example:

Increase bottom-line profits by 13% by March 30, 2017.

Profitable

If you ever want to measure the inefficiency of your time, or that of your team, ask them to participate in this simple exercise: Have them take a sheet of paper and draw a line down the middle. For a single day, have them track their activities by writing the activity on the left side of the page. On the right side, have them link that activity to how it directly creates revenue for the organization. For instance, they may write '30 minutes, answering emails' on the left side of the sheet. On the right side of that line, they may write 'following up with leads generates meetings which generates possible sales.' If you or your people cannot connect all of their activities with generating revenue within at least four steps, you'll know the activity isn't generating direct revenue. In fact, it may fall under the dreaded banner of 'busywork.'

Of course, the larger an organization is, the more removed some tasks become from directly generating revenue. A skilled leader with a strategic view of the organization can, however, explain how refilling the copy machine allows salespeople to be able to hand design schematics to the very clients that sign the checks. The more disconnected any task is in an employee's mind from generating revenue or fulfilling the organization's purpose, the less engaged they will be in completing it.

For instance, in one organization I worked with, employees had to fill out two versions of electronic timesheets each week. These redundant timesheets each required separate login usernames and passwords. Then employees also had to spend between twenty and sixty minutes each week accounting for every minute they spent at work, on leave, or off-duty, working without pay. Employees dreaded this part of their duties, and even though it was directly related to their pay, management struggled each week to get the timesheets turned in on time.

Why? No one could link the redundant timesheets to generating profit for the organization or to fulfilling its purpose. When management finally combined the timesheets into one system and educated people on how disbursing funds to payroll on time directly contributed to shareholder return, suddenly timesheet compliance jumped to near 100% each week.

Examine your current business objectives and the ones you plan moving forward using this same litmus test – does this business objective directly generate revenue for my organization? The sub-tasks beneath it may have a secondary or tertiary effect on revenue, but the profitability of your primary objectives should be very simple for any employee to understand, whether they are on the cleaning staff or in the executive suite. Tie each objective to directly benefitting the organization's purpose and/or bottom line:

Bad Profitability Example:

Increase speed of delivery.

Pivot Point Example:

Reduce round-trip delivery average to 1.5 hours per delivery/installation.

Purpose

Closely behind profit for any high-performing organization is purpose. While it is beyond the scope of this work to identify your organization's purpose, it is vital that every one of your business objectives is not only tied to profiting your business, but is also in line with its purpose.

Why is this important? The quickest way to have an employee de-prioritize any task is to make it feel like busywork to them. That happens if people can't connect the objective they're striving for to why their organization exists. Some organizations exist for the sole purpose of making a profit, and that's fine. If that's the case, every objective in your organization has to be hyper-focused on generating revenue. However, most business have more altruistic purposes at their foundation, such as family, community improvement, relieving pain for their customers, improving the quality of life of their employees/clients, and so on.

The key to creating business objectives that your teams will support, believe in and buy from comes down to connecting each business objective to your purpose or values. If your teams support your company's purpose and clearly understand how their business objectives align with that purpose, you have a much higher chance of them innovating solutions around challenges they might face. At that purpose-connected level, objectives become a mission that they will work to create, support and achieve.

Bad Purpose Example:

Get the furniture installed at the client's site.

Pivot Point Example:

Deliver the tools our clients need to improve their world.

Taken together, a business objective that is precise, profitable and in line with your purpose becomes something that prepares you to deal with unforeseen change and is something people will believe in and buy from.

Bad Overall Business Objective:

Increase profits in second quarter by speeding up delivery of furniture to clients.

Pivot Point Business Objective:

By March 31, 2017 we will maintain a margin of at least 4.5% by increasing speed of delivery to an average of 1.5 hours per install so our clients have the tools they need to improve their worlds.

Prepare – Alignment and Action

Once a clear business objective is in place, how do we prepare our people in a way that prevents unexpected events from derailing our objectives? We've seen the value that comes with preparation throughout the book, but how do we get our people as ready as possible to deal with inevitable challenges? There are two parts to preparation: Alignment and Action. Each of them is necessary to carry your plan to performance.

Alignment

The value of alignment cannot be understated, and anyone who has managed multiple teams knows the pain of what happens when the actions of one team or group of people is misaligned with those of another. However, alignment differs from purpose. Purpose deals with the core of a business, the why of what it does for its shareholders, employees and the world. Alignment, on the other hand, is the collective action of the people responsible for bringing purpose into being. Purpose can exist without alignment – but is much more difficult to fulfill without aligned action. Similarly, it is possible to align people around a common goal without giving them a purpose. The danger in that situation is a group of people who are pulling together in a direction that may not be best for the organization's long-term goals.

So how do we prepare our people and get them aligned in the same direction?

Much like you would talk with your teams and connect your business objectives to your organization's purpose, you must also connect your teams to your organization's long-term objectives. Only when each employee understands how the business objective they are pursuing this week, month and quarter fits in with the organization's long-term goals will they be aligned. Surprisingly, this is a part of management that leaders often ignore. In the majority of companies I work with, employees can't tell me what the specific long-range goals of their organization are. I'm lucky if I even get 'to make more money than we're making now' as a response. Sad as it may seem, the sadder fact is without a clear vision of where their organization aims to be five or ten years down the road, the employee doesn't know to be on the lookout for innovate ways to overcome challenges. The very people who are best poised to improve the way your business does business – those on the front lines – don't know what they're supposed to be improving or innovating toward.

Aligning your people to your short- and long-term business objectives is as simple as taking a few minutes to explain to your teams what your short and long-term business objectives are. Then encourage them to look for ways to move the needle of your organization toward them. After that, they can report their ideas to your team leads or whatever other continuous improvement channel you have. If you currently don't have a continuous improvement process or channel, we'll get to how to create one shortly.

As you've undoubtedly noticed, creating a Pivot Point involves moving from the macro to the micro again and again. First, you'll align your people on the larger business objectives you have – those that would fit under the term 'strategy.' You then need to align your people on the actions they'll need to complete today, this week and this month to achieve their part of their team's business objective. We'll use the house-clearing example we presented before and then explain how to prepare your folks for the things they'll do to bring your objectives into reality: the actions.

Action

When preparing military personnel for a mission with a clear objective, it's vital that every team member understand what action they will responsible for performing, what time that will need to occur, and what the result of their actions should look like. In a group of Marines preparing to clear a house, for instance, there is a Marine to gain entry into the building, a group of Marines to enter behind him or her and Marines assigned to cover a rotating sector of fire. These sectors change as Marines peel off into rooms to 'clear' them. Each Marine has to know not only what they are responsible for doing in the process, but also what each of their teammates is responsible for. They count on each other to protect the vulnerable areas of their squad as they move through a structure. Contrary to what Hollywood would have you believe, Marines would never dream of gathering outside a building and saying 'let's charge in there and give 'em hell!'

Instead, they carefully plan who will be first, second, third, etc. as they enter the structure, what sector of fire each position of their formation will be responsible for covering and at what specific times. If you could freeze a group of Marines performing this maneuver, you could ask any one of them what their role at that moment was and what their teammates were responsible for achieving as well. Because of their comprehensive understanding of who was responsible for performing a specific function, they can operate as a cohesive team and overcome pop-up changes to their plan. How do you achieve that level of teamwork in your organization?

Let's look at the business objective we created in our 'Planning' stage:

By March 31, 2017 we will increase bottom-line profits 13% by increasing speed of delivery to an average of 1.5 hours per install so our clients have the tools they need to improve their worlds.

To accomplish this, let's say we'll be dealing with a delivery crew of seven men and women. They travel in a truck to client sites. As we examine how to increase their efficiency to 1.5 hours per delivery, we realize that we currently have a lot of duplicated effort and wasted time among the crew members. When we gather our teams in the planning session, we'll want them to plan out how they could most efficiently assign roles, communicate with the client, unload the truck, assemble the product, remove waste materials and clean the client site. Once they have a process in place, it's important that every team member understand who is responsible for doing what, by when. A simple chart may look like this:

Order	Role	Task	Responsibility
1	Driver	Park vehicle in place that allows for easy unloading	Safely deliver product to client site
2	Lead Installer	Make contact with client, recon install sites	To ensure great client experience
3	Senior Installer	Supervise unloading of product and quality check assembly	Ensure product goes to correct location
4	Junior Installer 1	Unload product, assemble, remove waste	Ensure proper assembly of product and waste removal
5	Junior Installer 2	Unload product, assemble, remove waste	Ensure proper assembly of product and waste removal
6	Junior Installer 3	Unload product, assemble, remove waste	Ensure proper assembly of product and waste removal
7	Junior Installer 4	Unload product, assemble, clean all install sites of debris	Ensure proper assembly of product and clean client site

Of course, if you are a sole operator or part of a smaller team, you can easily adapt a simple matrix like the one above for your needs. The important things are to understand who will perform what function at one time and to have a clear idea of what the task will look like when completed. This is how pit crews in NASCAR train, and it is also what makes the military effective at building high-performing teams.

During training sessions, and again before leaving their warehouse, this crew would review what role each of them had been assigned. They would also have the opportunity to ask clarifying questions about possible challenges before getting in the trucks and arriving at the client site. Again, our objective is to make the delivery teams more efficient. We want everyone to understand what role they and the rest of their teammates will play so when they are executing on their objective it's all business. If something becomes a safety risk or could lead to an unhappy client, team members are empowered to bring it to their leader. Otherwise, feedback on their roles or duties can wait until they process after the completed install. Last-minute changes that normally derail such a team will have minimal effect because key members will know to mitigate and eliminate the risks these changes have to their success. Those roles are built into the chart they create and review before executing their objective.

Perform – Train, Target Acquisition and Use the Toolbox

If you've taken the time to plan a business objective that is precise, profitable and in line with your organization's purpose and then prepared your folks by aligning them, you've done more than 99% of the organizations in your industry. However, now your people are in the field, client-facing with your brand on the line. At this point, it is more important than ever they overcome last-minute changes and ensure your business objectives are achieved. To do that inside of any Pivot Point you are creating in your organization, you'll need to have two things – Training and a Toolbox.

Train

Wait, why is training part of performance and not preparation or planning? Great question. In many organizations, training is a function that happens when an employee is brought on board, proves minimal proficiency and then is released upon the organization's internal and external clients. Oftentimes, any training that occurs after that is the result of experience, and there's no guarantee that a positive or negative experience in the field will result in a change in behavior. Obviously, when we consider a job field where mistakes cost lives – not just in the military, but in healthcare, construction, etc. – being 'good enough' is no longer good enough.

For this reason, the military, and some other organizations, include training not just as part of their onboarding process, but also as part of their ongoing professional development. Many businesses have mapped career progressions that include professional development courses and advanced technical training. That's great for those on an upward climb, but what about organizations with limited upward or lateral mobility? How do we train our new people and ensure they continue to overcome changes to their plans?

The military solved this problem by establishing a basic method of training their people called 'Demo-Do.' It is essentially a micro-version of Pivot Point, where the leadership decides what the long-range objectives are for each individual role and then works to develop the training necessary for people to meet those objectives. This differs from the way most organizations train their people because 'Demo-Do' training actually trains people for what the organizations wants them to be able to perform in the future, rather than simply getting them to a medium level of proficiency based upon current performance rates. After all, don't we want to be part of an organization that is better tomorrow than it is today?

Once the long-range performance objective has been identified, the candidate is then shown how to perform the objective by an experienced member of the team. Usually, they are not shown more than a few times, even for extremely complex tasks. Again, this differs from most organizations that give people an almost unlimited amount of chances to witness a task before they ask their junior people to attempt it. It is a very

164

much 'up-or-out' system. While that may strike many leaders as harsh, ask yourself: If I show someone how to do something, explain it to them and then give them a chance to perform the task and they still botch it, is that really the right position for them?

We've mentioned that mistakes in the military mean life and death. Mistakes in how your people perform – from administrative functions to client-facing ones – mean the life and death of your organization, so the 'Demo-Do' process is worth taking seriously. Once a trainee has proved proficiency with a task, they are then sent into the field to perform it in a real world environment. Usually, this is done with an instructor watching. The instructor will only intervene if safety becomes an issue. After the task is completed to standard (or not), the instructor will then debrief the student on what they can do better. Only then is the trainee given the stamp of approval. If it's not performed to standard, the trainee is cycled back through training or moved to another position.

If the 'Demo-Do' process is how new skills are acquired, how do we continue to raise the bar on people who are already proficient? This involves taking the action items from your after-action reports and updating your standards. The new action items, learned from either failures or wins, then become the new proficiencies even the most experienced team members are expected to learn and perform.

One danger to be aware of is the 'salty veteran' mentality that often occurs among senior team members. In effect, their experience gives them blinders to innovation because 'that's the way we've always done that, and it works, so why change it?' This attitude can halt a training or continuous improvement program in its tracks. Because junior team members cannot be expected to perform to a standard higher than their senior team members are held to, even the best feedback will be useless if it isn't incorporated into policy. Those improvements, like all standards, must be supported and upheld by the leadership of your organization.

"Training junior members and improving the performance of my senior ones is important," I hear many leaders say, "but where am I supposed to find the time to do that amid the hundreds of other tasks they have to complete?"

This is a question that leaders of any size organization must contend with. Whether they are sole proprietors or executives in a multinational conglomerate, each must ask: How do we deal with task overload so our people make time for the most important things? The military uses a unique system to keep first things first, and that's what we will cover next.

Target Acquisition

The second element of performance after training is target acquisition. This is the method that infantry troops are taught in order to track multiple targets, while maintaining primary focus on the biggest 'threat' or 'opportunity.' Just as with a business, on the battlefield there are many moving targets people have to keep track of. Whether your teams are 'spinning' five plates or twenty, they still have to ensure that each important role they are responsible for is handled.

When learning basic infantry tactics, troops are given a 'primary target.' This is the biggest threat or opportunity for advancement available to them at any given time. It may be the closest threat, and therefore, the most dangerous to them, or it may be their mission objective. Wherever the threat falls in their view, they know to keep an almost-constant focus on it. In addition to that, they also have many more targets they have to ensure don't become primary targets or threats. There is always more than one target they must track. How do these men and women, in some of the most stressful environments on the planet, keep track of multiple targets? They use a simple system we'll call 'target acquisition.' Let's apply it to your organization so you can get your teams performing even when they have multiple roles and goals they have to achieve.

First, decide what the person/team/division's 'primary target' is. For many organizations, it's simple: Sales. Generate revenue. Obviously, that keeps the lights on. However, if all anyone in your business did was sell, who would process or deliver the orders? Who would follow up with current and former clients? Who would perform the hundreds or thousands of other jobs that have to be done to support the salespeople? In today's fast-paced business world, each employee plays multiple roles and is responsible for delivering across a variety of duties. If they are lucky enough to be responsible for directly generating revenue for your organization, then obviously 'sales' would be their primary target. Each employee, each member of your team, needs to know what their primary target is so they know what to pay the most attention to. But what to do with the sometimes dozens of other duties (secondary targets, tertiary targets, etc.) they're responsible for delivering on? This is where the target acquisition system comes in.

Troops begin and end their focus with the biggest challenge on their radar. It is the space in between those points of singular focus where they deal with all the other targets in their sights. For instance, your salespeople may have a primary target of 'sales' but secondary and tertiary targets of 'follow-up' and 'prospecting.' There may be a dozen more, but let's stick with those three for now: Sales, follow-up, prospecting.

Using a system of target acquisition, they would dive into sales and make sure all the duties they could handle at this time under that role were covered. Only then would they move over to their duties in follow-up and knock them out. When those are done, they don't move down to the next thing on their to-do list, because that next thing isn't their primary target!

Instead, they move right back to checking on their sales activities, their primary target. Only when that is handled do they move to their tertiary target, prospecting. They do as much as they can to move prospecting forward and then go right back to sales.

In this way, they are keeping first things first by tracking that all-important target: their primary one. This system can be used across a dozen duties or 'roles' to make sure each is receiving the attention they need and never letting the 'primary target' slip away from them. While this works as an excellent system individually among your team members, what happens in the likely scenario that members of your teams play time-sensitive, multiple roles? That is where bringing in the third element of performance, a Toolbox, comes in.

Use the Toolbox

The military is famous for having people serve in a wide variety of roles, each requiring specialized training. When a team needs a demolitions expert, they look for a combat engineer, not a cook in the mess hall. And when a unit is returning from the field and needs a hot meal, they don't wake up the combat engineers to get the grill going (unless people like crispy steaks!). Each role is specialized to perform a certain task at a certain time in order to move the organization's objectives forward.

In a small-team environment, each person will have a basic understanding of the roles to be performed and will also specialize in a certain skillset. For instance, in an infantry squad, there will be fire-team leaders (in a leadership role), machine-gunners, machine gunner assistants (to provide ammunition) and riflemen (to provide maneuvering and covering fire). Each person on the team is familiar enough with the team's goals to be able to handle a rifle, but when heavy firepower is needed, the machine gunner knows to step up. Conversely, if someone needs to move quickly through the alleys of a neighborhood, they won't send a machine gunner loaded with a hundred pounds of ammunition and a 20+ pound weapon. They'll send a rifleman who can move nimbly. The squad has developed a toolbox where each role plays a specific and critical part.

Similarly, organizations usually have 'toolboxes' of skillsets among their team members. The thing that makes Marines and other troops so effective in utilizing their toolbox is that they understand the timing and capability of the roles in their teams. When your folks are performing their duties, not only do they need to be well-trained and use target acquisition, they also need to know which specific skillset will need to come into play in order to achieve their business objective. Similarly, NASCAR pit crews invest a lot of time and resources to develop an almost-scientific formula for knowing when each of their team members needs to step in to provide their unique skillset to accomplish their objectives.

Using the toolbox of skillsets among your teams means you have the right person on hand to deal with the specific challenge you're facing at any given moment. As a leader, you can identify skillsets and timing when developing your plans in the planning stage of creating a Pivot Point. Using simulated and real-world training, you can have your teams practice using their various roles so they know who is responsible for performing what specialized task at a certain time. In this way, each of the skillsets you've invested in can be maximized to overcome any change you may encounter.

After your teams have executed on their objective, they now have an opportunity to sharpen their saws, examine their target acquisition systems, and ensure they are bringing the right skillsets to the table. They do this by processing their plans.

Process

Perhaps the most valuable and under-utilized of the 4 Ps of Pivot Point, processing with your teams after every mission they return from means the difference between repeating the same mistakes or settling for mediocre success and drastic improvement. Many companies wonder how their competition was able to outsmart, out-innovate and overtake them. While those can be organic processes in many high-performing organizations, they are also patterns that you can engineer into the way you do business.

When I was embedded in Marine Corps units around the world, it always surprised me that after a mission, no matter how tired, beat-up or (sometimes) bloody we were, we always took the time to stop and report on the mission we had just completed. Depending on the importance of the mission, sometimes it was a facilitated process and other times it was an informal chat, but it always occurred. Why? It was how we stayed a step ahead of our competition, and surprisingly, ourselves.

As you can imagine, competition on a battlefield is fierce. Everyone is carrying weapons designed by brilliant engineers to do incredible damage.

Our government invested hundreds of thousands of dollars in our training, and our competition may have been fighting in their home environment their entire lives. With modern technology, everyone on the battlefield has access to a video camera, and both sides are monitoring reports of how the other is fighting. In the same way, competition in your industry is likely just as intense. You and your competitors are selling similar products and services, but you must convince your prospects that yours are superior. Your organization has invested time in your training and in marketing your product or service. Likely, you and your competition are reading the same trade journals, attending the same industry events, and targeting the same clients. How can you stay a step ahead of your competition in an environment like that? You have to conduct after-action reports on your business objectives.

The value of processing our missions in the military was two-fold. First, we learned from every innovative idea any of the people in our organization had. When one of us invented or learned something that helped us mitigate or eliminate a last-minute change or challenge, it was immediately shared. Second, our competition could only use a tactic on any of us once. Imagine if your salespeople could only be out-sold by your competition for a certain reason once. You immediately prepared a plan to deal with that challenge in the future. What would that do to your revenue? For troops on the battlefield, whenever our enemy used a new tactic on us, a new maneuver, or a new weapon, we would include that in our after-action report. Most of the time we found a way to counter it and passed that information on so other units could react more quickly if they encountered the threat. On the rare cases we were overwhelmed by the new change to our plans, our leaders would immediately go to work innovating a solution for us that would be tested as soon as possible. If it worked, it would become standard policy and we would be trained to use it. Because we used a global database to store our after-action lessons, when we solved a problem the solution was immediately available for our teammates around the world. None of that would have been possible without a way to process our missions.

How do you leverage this incredibly valuable tool, even though you're not looking to create a global database but rather a continuous improvement program? The first place to start, as we've gone over, is having a clear business objective. Even the most expert facilitator will come up short when running an after-action around an objective as vague as 'earn more revenue.' However, with a business objective as specific as, 'By March 31, 2017 we will maintain a bottom-line profit of at least 13% by increasing speed of delivery to an average of 1.5 hours per install so our clients have the tools they need to improve their worlds,' we can learn what went right, what changes we encountered, and how to do things differently in the future. For businesses, the after-action method comes down to four simple questions:

What worked/didn't work in relation to our objective?

Once you review your objective with your team, the first question is not 'did we achieve our objective?' Not only is that a moot point (as your team will likely know the answer already), but it also encourages finger-pointing or back-slapping, neither of which is helpful in gathering usable lessons. Instead, ask your team: What worked in relation to executing our objective? Capture the answers on a whiteboard, pad of paper, or whatever you have available. A facilitation technique used in the military is for the leader to call themselves on the carpet first – this sets an open tone for junior members. If a leader is honest enough to admit what they did wrong, junior members can be as well. When you've had your folks data-dump their feedback, ask them to vote on the most useful things that contributed to getting them closer the business objective even if it wasn't achieved. You want to ask this because if there was something someone did out of the ordinary that did move the needle in the right direction, you want to capture that.

Next, repeat the process for: What didn't work in relation to our objective? Notice, the question was not 'who didn't do their job?' but rather 'what didn't work?' Even if a single team member caused the objective to fail, as a leader you're more interested in making sure no one else repeats the mistake. Counseling can occur offline for individuals. Capture the information and again have the team vote on the biggest contributor.

What's the reason it worked/didn't work?

Using the top five or six causes your team voted on, ask them 'what's the reason that worked?' It's very important that you don't settle for top-level answers here, because they usually aren't actionable. For instance, if someone says, 'That worked because we communicated well,' that's nice, but won't help your team in the future. Ask 'Why?' a few times until a solid, actionable answer appears. The conversation may look like this:

We got the install completed on time. Why did that work so well?

We communicated pretty well.

Why did we communicate well?

Well, we each knew what order things had to happen in.

Why were we all clear on the order of things?

We had gone over it in our prep session before leaving the warehouse.

It is that last item, prepping the order of installation before leaving the warehouse, that becomes an action item to include in the after-action report and build into future planning. If the action item is something that is already part of policy, that's fine. It is likely that between the 2-3 items you captured for 'what worked' in the first step, you'll find a new item to explore adding into your standards. When considering 'what's the reason it didn't work?' you might consider adding 'as well as it should have,' especially if your team reached their objective. That way, you're looking for things to improve upon while recognizing the team's high level of performance.

Who will change benefit?

This next question is important, because it will determine the value of your lesson. When you have your action items from both wins and losses, it's important to determine, 'Who in my company will benefit from making this the way we do business?' In most cases, making a change to the way your teams operate will have a trickle-down effect on many other departments. For instance, prepping the delivery teams so they finish installs on schedule doesn't just benefit the delivery team. It also benefits the customer in terms of satisfaction, potential of referring your organization to their associates, and repeat business. It also benefits the warehouse crew when they can depend on the trucks to get back on time and can prep the next day's deliveries. The salesperson will likely gain commissions generated from repeat business. The finance office will appreciate the fact that the margin is higher on a job completed in a timely manner. The list of benefits to partners – both external and internal – goes on and on. This question needs to be asked is because implementing change in any system is met with resistance. The way to overcome that resistance is to clearly identify how that change will add value not just to the people it directly affects, but to as many parts of the organization as possible.

What do we need to start doing differently, and when will it start?

This last question is where the rubber meets the road on Processing your business objectives. It is also where most organizations fail to take advantage of their wins and their losses. In most of the organizations I've worked with, teams are full of lessons learned, as well as the actionable items they have learned through hard work and experience. Unfortunately, these action items are rarely shared or implemented as policy. That means each team, and each employee, must deal with each change as if it is the first time it's ever occurred. This does a massive disservice to your junior team members. Again, the reason after-action reports work so well in the military is not just because the lessons are extracted after each mission – they're valuable because they are used in the next planning and preparing sessions.

When you have captured your action items from your after-action meeting, assign the action item to a timeline and an implementation date. While most of your action items will be immediately implementable, there will be a few situations that require further research and planning, such as implementing new technology, hiring new personnel, etc. In such cases, establish a clear timeline for when those items will be investigated and acted upon, and by whom. In this way, you can track your after-action items and ensure they're implemented. The fastest way to lose momentum in processing your business objectives is to take the time to meet and not use what you learned to improve your teams' performance.

CONCLUSION:
MAKING PIVOT POING PART OF YOUR CULTURE

We've covered a lot of ground in this book. In a very short amount of time, you've learned what it took the military centuries to piece together. You've learned how to collaboratively plan, lining up resources to deal with the risks you'll likely face. You've learned to identify who is going to do what by when, and to hold them accountable. You've learned how to prepare your teams and how to execute in challenging environments. You've learned how to implement a continuous improvement program into your operations so you continue to learn and stay a step ahead of your competition. Finally, you've seen how it all ties together to create a way to turn on a dime without sacrificing the results your organization counts on.

However, we're not ready for you to step out of the gate and create a Pivot Point that your organization can leverage. As we've covered, Pivot Point isn't just a management trick or a way to tweak performance in a few critical areas. Rather, it is a way of improving the processes in your business so change doesn't derail your goals, but accelerates them. Because it is such a drastically different way of operating for most companies who are 'just getting by,' it's worth going over the common bumps in the road you'll likely face from your leadership and from your teams as you begin to create a Pivot Point in the way you do business. Below are some of the comments I've heard from both start-ups and in some of the largest companies on the planet as they began creating Pivot Points for themselves.

Wait, we have a great culture now! Won't these 'military' processes make us all feel like robots?

When managers and employees hear that you'll be requiring them to use processes developed in the military —especially those that will hold them accountable for their performance – you're likely to get some pushback.

'We're not soldiers. Requiring everyone to do the same thing will make us robots.' It's a common misconception that service members are automatons, that they just do what they're told and can't think outside the box. Nothing could be further from the truth, especially in modern combat. When soldiers were trained to march onto the field of battle in formation, their most complicated actions consisting of marching in step, loading and firing their weapons, it made sense that they only focus on one thing at a time. Officers were the ones trained to think strategically. Today, the military consists of small teams. Even campaigns large enough to liberate countries are made up of individual units, each with a surgically-focused purpose and objective. The days of 'mindless soldiers' are over. The military regularly turns away those who can't think critically. When we consider the addition of technology that even the most basic infantryman is responsible for being able to operate and leverage, from drones to satellites, it's clear that critical thinking is not just a 'nice to have' on the battlefield, but a requirement.

More than that, the most valued skill in a challenging environment – whether on the battlefield or in business – is resourcefulness. From it comes innovation. Another critical element of the military's success comes from its ability to encourage resourcefulness among its employees and its ability to quickly share innovative solutions. The days of service members being 'robots' is officially over.

Creating a Pivot Point in your organization is taking the very best parts of the military's planning and execution processes and leveraging them to generate revenue, continuously improve, and leverage unexpected change. Of course, as you've seen, using these processes will greatly reduce the number of 'unexpected' changes your teams encounter. While this process has its roots in the military, it is adaptable to any industry from IT to manufacturing. As each organization I've worked with adopts it, Pivot Point takes on a new flavor, a new look and feel that fits in with the existing culture of the organization.

A related challenge comes from implementing new processes into an organization. Many companies are fiercely proud of the cultures they've organically or purposefully nurtured and don't want to lose the autonomy, freedom or communication their employees currently enjoy. They see creating a Pivot Point as something that will 'force' their people to do things differently. However, the elements of Pivot Point were developed across an organization with drastically different internal cultures – from the 'gung-ho' attitude of Marines to the 'work smarter, not harder' attitude of the Air Force. When I've worked with businesses to implement Pivot Points in their organizations, I've found that these processes don't change culture, but rather amplify it. If your teams are fiercely independent, they'll appreciate the autonomy that exists when managers trust their teams to get the job done. Managers will benefit because those teams are executing to specific objectives and continuously improving their performance. If your teams work well in a shared space and enjoy open communication, they'll benefit from the structure that Pivot Point gives to how they share information cross-team and cross-department.

If your organization is in a start-up phase or you are launching a new vertical, a concern may be that implementing processes will stymie your team's growth. After all, isn't creativity nurtured in an open environment where people can think 'outside the box'? There's no reason that innovation and creativity can't explode in a new organization using Pivot Point. The difference between a new team or organization using Pivot Point and one that doesn't is that the Pivot Point group will be able to quickly scale their operations and replicate their successes. The one that isn't using it will have to rely on assembling the exact personalities and skillsets all over again or promoting team members into leadership positions when they may not be ready/qualified to lead.

Creating a Pivot Point gives a new organization the foundation it can expand from.

We already have our own way of planning-preparing-performing-processing, and our folks don't want to change the way we do things.

If you have planning-preparing-performing-processing methods that are consistently used across all departments in your organization, count yourself among an extremely small group of businesses. Likely, you're already blowing past your competition and opening new market space. You may be asking: What could Pivot Point offer my high-performing team?

Whether your organization is using Six-Sigma, Agile methodologies, SCRUM, Kanban or any other system, you're encouraged to examine what parts of each of the 4 Ps you're not currently implementing and incorporate them into your existing process-management system. Pivot Point has been leveraged by Six Sigma Black Belts and SCRUM masters to amplify the results of their primary management systems and earn millions of dollars in additional revenue for their organizations. If you aren't using one of the 4 Ps, introduce it into your existing processes and let your folks tell you how to customize it for your organization.

Rather than competing with management systems and processes, Pivot Point serves as an adaptable structure that ties the strategy of your organization to the results that methodologies like Six Sigma and SCRUM produce. Both Pivot Point and other systems allow you to improve operations. However, creating a Pivot Point in your business allows you to give structure to and improve the way you handle unexpected change.

Pivot Point

Create a Pivot Point in the way you do business and it can be incorporated within all of your existing operational improvement methods.

I'm not a strategic leader, or I don't supervise a big team. How can I use Pivot Point in my department or on my own?

Because the elements of Pivot Point were adapted from the way both large armies and elite teams execute their objectives, Pivot Point is adaptable for campaigns involving hundreds of thousands of people and also for individuals. As you scale the principles of Pivot Point from large companies, remember that you're simply taking the principles from a macro to a micro level. Consider yourself a 'special forces' operator, someone who regularly has to do more with less. Create clear business objectives for your individual projects/business, review them before starting on your own each day, keep first things first, and do an after-action report on your own performance. When your supervisor sees your performance and results improve, give them a copy of this book. If you're a solopreneur, when your bottom line benefits from your results, share the book with your fellow entrepreneurs.

A FINAL STORY: YOURS

In the first part of this book, you learned the strategic mistakes most organizations make in dealing with change that eventually lead to them being overtaken by more nimble, agile competitors. You read the stories of those service members and businesspeople who were able to benefit from the principles of Pivot Point. From large organizations to small teams, you've learned how Pivot Point can be leveraged to deal with challenges that normally derail business objectives. You've read how this system developed over hundreds of years in the most challenging environments on the planet.

There's only one question that remains: Where will you take Pivot Point from here?

This system wasn't developed and tested in a static environment. It's changed as technology, people and marketplaces evolved. Whether your business objective is to remain profitable or to completely conquer your industry, implement the system you've learned here and adapt it to your organization's unique culture, people, geography, and customers. I'm excited to hear how Pivot Point is working in your organization – feel free to send your thoughts, ideas and stories to shawn@shoshinconsulting. com.

Training is over. It's time for you to take action on what you've learned.

Define a precise, profitable and purpose-driven objective and get started today on making your plans a reality.

Before Marines I served with left the safety of their bases and went outside the wire on patrol, they would wish each other good luck in the way only Marines could - a blessing for warriors confident in their ability to overcome any challenge they might face. I say the same blessing to you as you step out the gate to achieve your objectives:

Get Some.

ABOUT THE AUTHOR

Author photo by Kristina Houser, Photographer

Shawn Rhodes is a national expert on process and performance improvement in organizations. His two degrees, international study of organizational execution on-site in more than two dozen countries and multiple combat deployments as a Marine Corps War Correspondent prepared him for the battlefield of business. As president and founder of Shoshin Consulting, Shawn has consulted organizations ranging from Fortune 100 and 500 companies to tech start-ups and mom-and-pop companies. In 2014, Shawn was named one of the top 20 public speakers in the world by Toastmasters International. In addition to his hundreds of published articles, videos, podcasts and TEDx talk, Shawn and his work have been featured in TIME, CNN, NBC and hundreds of media outlets around the world.

To learn more about Shawn Rhodes and his other services, including keynotes, results-oriented process improvement and performance-enhancing consulting, please visit www.shoshinconsulting.com